STUDENT BOOK
with Self-Study Audio CD and CD-ROM

WorldView
2A

MICHAEL ROST

Simon le Maistre   **Carina Lewis**

Gillie Cunningham   **Sue Mohamed**   **Helen Solórzano**

Simon Greenall
Series Editor, British English edition

PEARSON
Longman

WorldView Student Book 2A with Self-Study Audio CD and CD-ROM

Authorized adaptation from the United Kingdom edition entitled *Language to Go*, First Edition, published by Pearson Education Limited publishing under its Longman imprint.
Copyright © 2002 by Pearson Education Limited

American English adaptation published by Pearson Education, Inc. Copyright © 2005.

Pearson Education, 10 Bank Street, White Plains, NY 10606

Editorial director: Pamela Fishman
Project manager: Irene Frankel
Senior development editors: Karen Davy, Stella Reilly
Vice president, director of design and production: Rhea Banker
Executive managing editor: Linda Moser
Associate managing editor: Mike Kemper
Production editor: Michael Mone
Art director: Elizabeth Carlson
Vice president, director of international marketing: Bruno Paul
Senior manufacturing buyer: Edie Pullman
Text and cover design: Elizabeth Carlson
Photo research: Aerin Csigay
Text composition: Word and Image Design
Text font: 10.5/13pt Utopia and 10/12pt Frutiger Bold

ISBN: 0-13-243300-1

Library of Congress Control Number: 2003115897

Printed in the United States of America
5 6 7 8 9 10–V003–09

Text Credits
Page 21 "River Deep, Mountain High." Jeff Barry, Ellie Greenwich and Phil Spector. © 1966, 1967 Trio Music Co., Inc., Mother Bertha Music, Inc. and Universal — Songs of Polygram International, Inc. (BMI). Copyrights renewed. All rights on behalf of Mother Bertha Music, Inc. administered by ABKCO Music, Inc. All rights reserved. Used by permission of Warner Bros. Publications. 59 "Wonderful Tonight." Words and Music by Eric Clapton. © 1977 by Eric Patrick Clapton. All rights in the U.S.A. Administered by Unichappell Music Inc. All rights reserved. Used by permission of Warner Bros. Publications.

Illustration Credits
Pierre Berthiaume, pp. 38, 57; Kasia Charko, pp. 64, 67; François Escalmel, p. 31; Stephen Harris, p. 63, 140, 142; Paul McCusker, pp. 18-19, 46-47; NSV Productions, pp. 138, 141; Stephen Quinlan, pp. 33, 137, 139.

Photo Credits
Page 3 *(top)* Doug Menuez/Getty Images, *(middle)* Cosmo Condina/Getty Images, *(bottom)* The Stock Market; 8 AbleStock/Index Stock Imagery; 10 Spencer Platt/Newsmakers/Getty Images; 11 *(top)* Aquarius Library, *(bottom)* Rex Features/SIPA; 12 Richard Smith/Corbis; 15 *(top right)* Stone/Stewart Cohen, *(middle left)* Stone/David Ball, *(middle right)* Pictor International, *(bottom left)* Ulli Seer/Getty Images, *(bottom right)* John W. Banagan/Getty Images; 16 *(top)* Peter Adams/Getty Images, *(bottom)* Stone/Lori Adamski Peek; 19 Arlene Sandler/SuperStock; 20 B.D.V./Corbis; 23 Ryan McVay/Getty Images; 26 *(top)* Graham Porter, *(middle)* Walter Hodges/Getty Images, *(bottom)* Getty Images; 27 Network Photographers; 28 Laurence Monneret/Getty Images; 30 *(left & right)* Ryan McVay/Getty Images; 31 *(left)* Amos Morgan/Getty Images, *(right)* Dorling Kindersley Media Library; 32 *(bottom)* Erik Dreyer/Getty Images; 34 *(A)* Danjaq/Eon/UA/The Kobal Collection, *(B)* Universal/The Kobal Collection/Bruce McBroom, *(C)* Moviestore Collection; 35 Moviestore Collection; 36 G.D.T./Getty Images; 39 Touchstone/The Kobal Collection; 40 Getty Images; 41 Tom Paiva/Getty Images; 44 *(A)* Hutchinson Library, *(B)* Science Photo Library, *(C)* Science Photo Library, *(D)* Corbis, *(E)* Science Photo Library, *(F)* Art Directors & Trip, *(G)* Katz Pictures; 48 *(top)* Getty Images, *(middle)* Getty Images, *(bottom)* Robert Harding Picture Library; 49 Getty Images; 50 Jose Luis Pelaez, Inc./Corbis; 52 Robert Harding Picture Library; 53 Getty Images; 54 Getty Images; 58 *(top)* Neal Preston/Corbis, *(left)* RubberBall Productions/Getty Images, *(middle)* Ryan McVay/Getty Images, *(right)* Digital Vision/Getty Images; 60 *(A)* Steve Cole/Getty Images, *(B)* Dorling Kindersley Media Library, *(C)* Barry Rosenthal/Getty Images, *(D)* Dorling Kindersley Media Library, *(E)* Getty Images, *(F)* Getty Images, *(G)* Liz McAulay/Dorling Kindersley Media Library, *(H)* Dorling Kindersley Media Library, *(I)* Stephen Oliver/Dorling Kindersley Media Library, *(J)* Steve Gorton/Dorling Kindersley Media Library; 62 Dorling Kindersley Media Library; 66 Adam Smith/Getty Images.

Introduction

Welcome to *WorldView*, a four-level English course for adults and young adults. *WorldView* builds fluency by exploring a wide range of compelling topics presented from an international perspective. A trademark two-page lesson design, with clear and attainable language goals, ensures that students feel a sense of accomplishment and increased self-confidence in every class.

WorldView's approach to language learning follows a simple and proven **MAP**:
- **M**otivate learning through stimulating content and achievable learning goals.
- **A**nchor language production with strong, focused language presentations.
- **P**ersonalize learning through engaging and communicative speaking activities.

Course components

The *WorldView Student Book with Self-Study Audio CD and WorldView To Go CD-ROM* and the *Workbook* are available in both full and split editions.

- **Student Book with Self-Study Audio CD and *WorldView* To Go CD-ROM** *(Split Edition)*
  The **Student Book** contains 14 four-page units; periodic Review Units; two World of Music Units; Information for Pair and Group Work; a Vocabulary list; and a Grammar Reference section.

  The **Self-Study Audio CD** includes tracks for all pronunciation and listening exercises (or reading texts, in selected units) in the *Student Book*. The *Self-Study Audio CD* can be used with the *Student Book* for self-study and coordinates with the *Workbook* listening and pronunciation exercises.

- The *WorldView* **To Go CD-ROM** offers a rich variety of interactive activities for each unit: vocabulary games, grammar exercises, and model conversations with record-and-compare and role-play features.

- The interleaved **Teacher's Edition** provides step-by-step procedures, exercise answer keys, and a wealth of teacher support: unit Warm-ups, Optional Activities, Extensions, Culture Notes, Background Information, Teaching Tips, Wrap-ups, and extensive Language Notes.

- The **Workbook** *(Split Edition)* has 14 three-page units that correspond to each of the *Student Book* units. Used in conjunction with the *Self-Study Audio CD*, the *Workbook* provides abundant review and practice activities for Vocabulary, Grammar, Listening, and Pronunciation, along with periodic Self-Quizzes. A Learning Strategies section at the beginning of the *Workbook* helps students to be active learners.

- The **Class Audio Program** is available in either CD or cassette format and contains all the recorded material for in-class use.

- The **Teacher's Resource Book** (with **Testing Audio CD** and **TestGen Software**) has three sections of reproducible material: extra communication activities for in-class use, model writing passages for each *Student Book* writing assignment, and a complete testing program: seven quizzes and two tests, along with scoring guides and answer keys. Also included are an Audio CD for use with the quizzes and tests and an easy-to-use TestGen software CD for customizing the tests.

- The *WorldView* **Video** presents fourteen one-to-four-minute authentic video segments connected to *Student Book* topics. The videos (VHS and DVD) come with a **Video/DVD Workbook and Guide** that includes Lesson Plans, Student Activity Sheets, and Teacher's Notes, all of which can also be downloaded from the *WorldView* **Companion Website.**

- The *WorldView* **Companion Website** (www.longman.com/worldview) provides a variety of teaching support, including model conversations, Video Activity Sheets, and supplemental reading material.

- The *WorldView* **Placement Test** helps teachers place students in the appropriate level of *WorldView*. The placement test package contains detailed instructions, an Audio CD and audioscripts, answer keys, sample essays, rubrics for the speaking and writing tests, and level placement tables.

Unit contents

Each of the units in *WorldView* has seven closely linked sections:
- **Getting started:** a communicative opening exercise that introduces target vocabulary
- **Listening/Reading:** a functional conversation or thematic passage that introduces target grammar
- **Grammar focus:** an exercise sequence that allows students to focus on the new grammar point and to solidify their learning
- **Pronunciation:** stress, rhythm, and intonation practice based on the target vocabulary and grammar
- **Speaking:** an interactive speaking task focused on student production of target vocabulary, grammar, and functional language
- **Writing:** a personalized writing activity that stimulates student production of target vocabulary and grammar
- **Conversation to go:** a concise reminder of the grammar and functional language introduced in the unit

Course length

With its flexible format and course components, *WorldView* responds to a variety of course needs, and is suitable for 35 to 45 hours of classroom instruction. Each unit can be easily expanded by using bonus activities from the *Teacher's Edition*, reproducible activities available in the *Teacher's Resource Book*, linked lessons from the *WorldView Video* program, and supplementary reading assignments in the *WorldView* Companion Website.

Scope and Sequence

GRAMMAR FOCUS	PRONUNCIATION	SPEAKING	WRITING
Review and expansion: simple present and adverbs of frequency	Sentence rhythm/stress	Talking about how often you do things	Describe your weekend routines and activities
Linking words: *and, but, so*	Intonation in sentences	Apologizing and making excuses	Write email messages apologizing and giving excuses
Simple past: regular and irregular verbs	*-ed* simple past ending	Talking about past events	Describe an important time or event in your life
be going to for future	Stress in names of countries	Talking about plans	Write a letter to a friend about a trip you plan to take
Modals: *should* and *shouldn't* for advice	Weak and strong forms: *should, shouldn't*	Giving advice	Write an email giving advice to a friend on what he or she should or shouldn't do while visiting your country
Expressions for making suggestions	Intonation: focus words	Making suggestions	Write email messages giving suggestions and advice about parties
be and *have* with descriptions	Weak forms: *and, or*	Describing people	Describe the physical appearance of a friend, family member, or famous person
say and *tell*	Consonant clusters	Talking about movies	Write a movie review
would like/like, would prefer/prefer	Weak and strong forms: *would, wouldn't*	Ordering food and drinks in a restaurant	Write a memo describing the food and drink items for a menu
will for predicting	Word stress	Making predictions	Creating a web page about five predictions for the year 2100
have to/don't have to	Have to (*hafta*) and has to (*hasta*)	Describing jobs	Describe a typical day in your ideal job
Present perfect for indefinite past: *ever, never*	Linking vowel to vowel (*have you ever, has she ever*)	Talking about practical experience	Write a letter explaining why you should be on a reality TV show
Review: possessive *'s*, possessive adjectives/ possessive pronouns; *belong to*	Stress and linking in phrasal verbs	Talking about special possessions	Describe a keepsake that belongs to you or a family member
Adverbs of manner; comparative adverbs	Stressed syllables and /ə/ in adverbs	Describing actions	Write a short story or folktale

It's the weekend!

Vocabulary Weekend activities
Grammar Simple present and adverbs of frequency
Speaking Talking about how often you do things

Getting started

Ⓐ

1 Look at the photos. What are the people doing?

2 Complete the sentences with the verb phrases in the boxes.

| go for a walk | ~~go to the beach~~ | go out for dinner |

1. I love Sundays. I _____*go to the beach*_____ on Sunday mornings. In the afternoon, I _____ in the park. Then I sometimes _____ with friends.

| go to the gym | stay home | sleep late | watch TV |

2. Saturday is my favorite day of the week. I _____ on Saturday mornings. I like to exercise, so I _____ in the afternoon. In the evenings, I _____ with my family and we _____ together.

| get takeout | go to the movies | work late |

3. It's Friday—almost the weekend! I _____ on Friday nights because I want to finish my work before the weekend. I don't like to cook, so I _____ on my way home. Then I _____ with friends.

3 **PAIRS.** Talk about the weekend activities in Exercise 2 that you like to do.

I like to sleep late, go to the movies, and go out for dinner.

Listening

4 🎧 **Listen to the radio program about how people around the world spend their weekend. Find the photo that each speaker describes.**

Speaker 1 (Yuka) ____   Speaker 2 (Marcelo) ____

5 🎧 **Listen again and underline the correct information.**

1. Yuka never **gets takeout** / **cooks** on Fridays.
2. She often **meets friends** / **stays home**.
3. She usually **goes to the movies** / **watches TV** with her friends.
4. Marcelo always goes **to the gym** / **to the beach** on Sundays.
5. He sometimes goes out for **lunch** / **dinner**.

Pronunciation

6 🎧 **Listen to the rhythm in the sentences. Notice that the important words are pronounced longer, clearer, and stronger than the other words.**

I **nev**er **work** on **Sat**urday.
I **u**sually **go** to the **gym**.

What do you **do** on **Sun**day?
We **go** for a **walk** on the **beach**.

She **al**ways gets **take**out on **Fri**days.
She **goes** to the **mov**ies with her **friends**.

7 🎧 **Listen again and repeat.**

B

C

Grammar focus

1 Write the adverbs of frequency in the correct place on the scale.

| always | never | often | ~~sometimes~~ | usually |

100% _____
|
_____
_____
_____sometimes_____
0% _____

2 Study the examples with adverbs of frequency.

> I **often work** late on Friday.
> He **always goes** to the beach on the weekend.
> The beach **is usually** crowded.

3 Look at the examples again. Circle the correct words to complete the rules in the chart.

> **Simple present and adverbs of frequency**
>
> The adverb of frequency comes **before / after** the verb *be*.
>
> The adverb of frequency comes **before / after** all other verbs.

Grammar Reference page 143

4 Complete the sentences with a verb and the adverb of frequency in parentheses.

1. A: Her husband _often works_ late on Fridays. Doesn't he? (often)

   B: No, never. He _____ to the movies with friends. (always)

2. A: What do you do on Saturday mornings?

   B: I _____ to the gym. (usually)

3. A: Do you usually go out on Saturday night?

   B: No. I _____ home. (usually)

4. A: How _____ do you _____ takeout for dinner? (often)

   B: I _____ takeout on Saturdays. (sometimes)

5. A: I _____ home on Sunday nights. Do you? (never)

   B: Yes. I _____ a video at home. (sometimes)

5 *PAIRS.* Practice the conversations in Exercise 4.

Speaking

6 *BEFORE YOU SPEAK.* Write five sentences about your weekend. Use each of the adverbs of frequency from Exercise 1.

I never go to the gym on Sundays.

7 *GROUPS OF 3.* Create a survey together. Each person, add one weekend activity to the survey form.

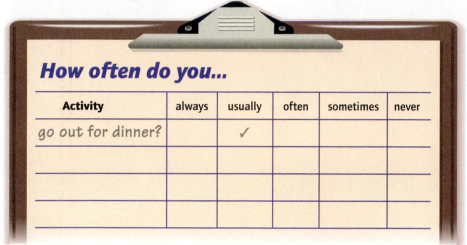

How often do you...

Activity	always	usually	often	sometimes	never
go out for dinner?		✓			

8 *GROUPS OF 3.* Take turns. Tell each other about your weekend activities. Use an adverb of frequency and give additional information. Check (✓) the box in the survey for each answer.

I usually go out for dinner on the weekend. I usually have Italian food.

9 *GROUPS OF 3.* Compare your weekends. Who has the most relaxing weekend? Who has the busiest weekend?

Writing

10 Imagine that your weekends are always perfect—you do only activities that you love. Write about your perfect weekends. What do you do? What don't you do? Use adverbs of frequency.

CONVERSATION TO GO

A: How **often** do you work late?
B: **Never!**

Excuses, excuses

Vocabulary Parts of the body; illnesses and injuries
Grammar Linking words: *and, but, so*
Speaking Apologizing and making excuses

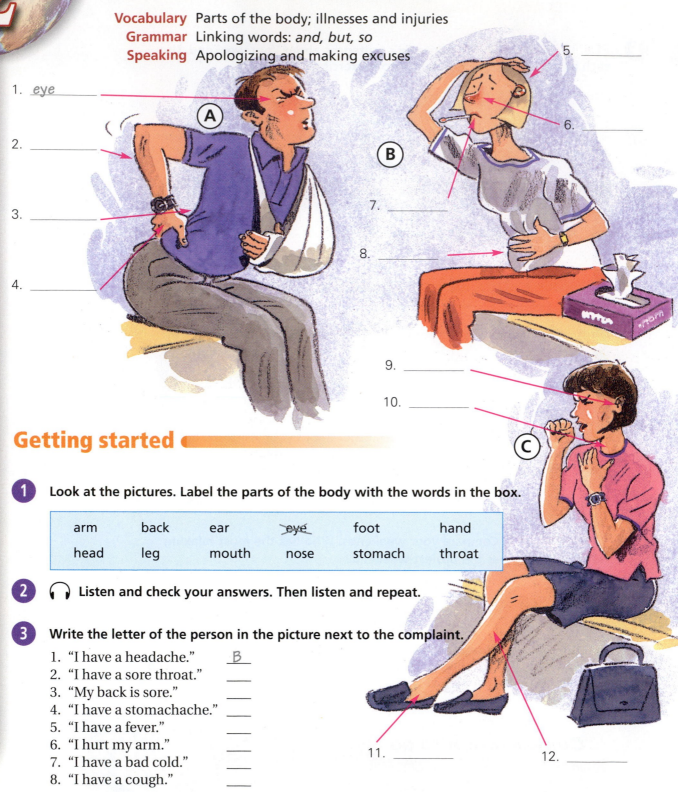

1. *eye*
2. _____
3. _____
4. _____

5. _____
6. _____
7. _____
8. _____
9. _____
10. _____
11. _____
12. _____

Getting started

1 Look at the pictures. Label the parts of the body with the words in the box.

arm	back	ear	~~eye~~	foot	hand
head	leg	mouth	nose	stomach	throat

2 🎧 Listen and check your answers. Then listen and repeat.

3 Write the letter of the person in the picture next to the complaint.

1. "I have a headache."   _B_
2. "I have a sore throat."   ___
3. "My back is sore."   ___
4. "I have a stomachache."   ___
5. "I have a fever."   ___
6. "I hurt my arm."   ___
7. "I have a bad cold."   ___
8. "I have a cough."   ___

4 *PAIRS.* Test your partner on the names of illnesses and injuries. Student A, point to a part of your body and act out the problem (for example, touch your throat). Student B, say the problem (for example: *Oh, you have a sore throat!*).

Listening

5 🎧 **Listen to Tony tell his boss, Roger, why he can't come to work. Put his excuses in the correct order.**

____ He has a cough and a sore throat.

____ He hurt his back.

__1__ He has a fever.

____ He has a stomachache.

6 🎧 **What does Tony say to apologize? How does Roger respond? Listen again. Match Tony's apologies with Roger's responses.**

Apology	Sympathetic response
1. ____ I'm really sorry, but . . .	a. That's OK. Hope you get better soon.
2. ____ I'm afraid I can't . . .	b. That's too bad.
3. ____ I'm sorry, but . . .	c. That's OK. Don't worry.

7 *PAIRS.* **Take turns. Student A, use the ideas below and the complaints from Exercise 3 to apologize and make an excuse. Student B, give a sympathetic response.**

A: *I'm sorry, but I can't come to work today. I have a fever.*
B: *That's OK. Hope you get better soon.*

Apology

I'm afraid . . .

I'm sorry, but . . .

I'm really sorry, but . . .

I can't play soccer today.
I can't give my report today.
I can't go out for dinner with you.
I can't come to work today.
I can't help you lift that box.
I can't sign my name on the check.
I can't do my homework.

Grammar focus

1 Study the examples with the linking words *and, but,* and *so.*

> I have a bad cough, **and** my throat is very sore.
> I can't come in today, **but** I'll probably be there tomorrow.
> I have a fever, **so** I can't come to work today.

2 Look at the examples again. Complete the rules in the chart with *and, but,* or *so.*

Linking words: *and, but, so*
Use _____ to add a similar idea.
Use _____ to add a different idea.
Use _____ to show the result of something.

> *Grammar Reference page 143*

3 Combine the sentences with the linking words in parentheses.

1. She hurt her arm. She can't use the computer. (so)

   She hurt her arm, so she can't use the computer.

2. I have a cough. I don't have a sore throat. (but)

3. My father hurt his back. My brother hurt his leg. (and)

4. I have a stomachache. I'm going to stay home. (so)

5. She doesn't have a fever. She feels sick. (but)

6. He has a headache. I gave him some aspirin. (so)

Pronunciation

4 🎧 Listen. Notice the way the voice goes up on the most important word in each part of the sentence, and then down.

I'm **sor**ry,   but I have a **cold**.

I have a **cough**,   and my **throat** is sore.

I'm really **sor**ry,   but I'm not **feel**ing very well.

I have a **fev**er,   so I can't come to **work**.

5 🎧 Listen again and repeat.

Speaking

6 **PAIRS.** Take turns apologizing and making excuses using the expressions below. Student A, look at page 136. Student B, look at page 138.

Apologize	Show sympathy
I'm (really) sorry, but . . .	That's OK.
I'm afraid . . .	Don't worry.
	That's too bad!

A: *I'm afraid I can't come to work. I have a terrible headache.*
B: *That's too bad!*

Writing

7 You don't feel well today. Reply to each email message. Give an apology and an excuse.

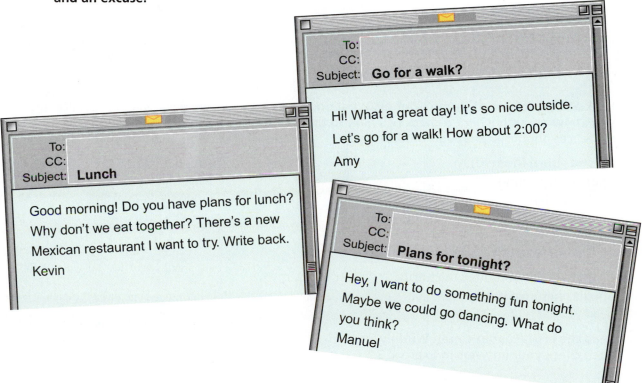

To:
CC:
Subject: **Go for a walk?**

Hi! What a great day! It's so nice outside.
Let's go for a walk! How about 2:00?

Amy

To:
CC:
Subject: **Lunch**

Good morning! Do you have plans for lunch? Why don't we eat together? There's a new Mexican restaurant I want to try. Write back.

Kevin

To:
CC:
Subject: **Plans for tonight?**

Hey, I want to do something fun tonight. Maybe we could go dancing. What do you think?

Manuel

CONVERSATION TO GO

A: **I'm afraid** I can't come to work. I have a sore throat, and I can't talk.
B: **That's too bad!**

A life of achievement

Vocabulary Life events
Grammar Simple past: regular and irregular verbs
Speaking Talking about past events

Getting started

1 **Number the life events in the order they usually occur.**

have children ___	find a job ___	graduate from school ___
get married ___	grow up ___	go to school ___
work hard ___	be born _1_	

2 *PAIRS.* **Compare your answers.**

Reading

3 **Look at the pictures of Oprah Winfrey. What do you know about her? Put a check (✓) next to the sentences about her that you think are true.**

She was born in the U.S.
She's an only child.
She's married.
She lives in an apartment in Chicago.
She has a plane.
She doesn't have children.
She gives a lot of money to charity.
She has her own magazine.

4 **Read the article about Oprah Winfrey. Then check your answers in Exercise 3.**

5 *PAIRS.* **Discuss. Did anything in the article surprise you?**

Oprah Winfrey

People in more than 132 countries watch *Oprah*. On this TV talk show, ordinary people talk about their problems and Oprah Winfrey helps them.

Oprah lives in a wonderful apartment in Chicago and has a farm and a house in the mountains. She has great cars and a plane too. But Oprah Winfrey was not always rich and famous.

① Oprah Winfrey was born.

② She left college.

③ She had her first talk show.

④ She started *The Oprah Winfrey Show.*

⑤ She acted in her first movie.

1954

What kind of life did Oprah have as a child?

Oprah Winfrey was born in 1954 in Mississippi, in the U.S. Her family didn't have a lot of money. Oprah could read and write when she was three, and she loved books. She worked hard and was an excellent student at school, but she left college in 1973 when she was nineteen and didn't finish her education.

How did she start her successful career?

Oprah wanted to be famous, and her dream came true when she found a job in TV. She was the first woman and the first black newscaster on TV in Nashville, Tennessee. In 1977, she had her first TV talk show. In 1984, she moved to Chicago and started *The Oprah Winfrey Show*. It was a great success.

Oprah in *The Color Purple*

What did she do later?

In 1985, Oprah acted in Steven Spielberg's movie *The Color Purple*. After that, she made several other popular films. She didn't have any children, but she used her success to help other people's children. In 1997, she started a charity called Oprah's Angel Network. In the first five years, the charity collected more than $12 million and gave it to people in need. Oprah's Angel Network helps students to go to college, poor families to build their own homes, and communities to become safer. Oprah began her own magazine for women in the spring of 2000. It's simply called *O*. The magazine contains many personal stories and moving articles that reflect her interest in helping people worldwide. Her television program is still very popular, but now it's just called *Oprah*.

6 Read the article again. Then write the correct years on the timeline.

7 She started her own magazine.

6 She started a charity to help other people.

Grammar focus

1 **Study the examples of regular and irregular verbs in the simple past.**

Regular verbs	Irregular verbs
Examples: *love, work, finish, end, want, move, act, start*	Examples: *be, can, leave, find, do, give, have*
(?) How **did** she **start** her successful career? **(?) Did** she **start** acting right away? **(+)** She **started** *The Oprah Winfrey Show* in 1984. **(–)** She **didn't start** the Angel Network in 1984.	What kind of life **did** she **have** as a child? **Did** she **have** any brothers and sisters? She **had** her first talk show in 1977. Her family **didn't have** a lot of money.

2 **Look at the examples again. Is the rule in the chart true (*T*) or false (*F*)?**

Simple past: regular and irregular verbs
Use the simple past to talk about completed actions in the past. _____

> *Grammar Reference page 143*

3 **Complete the story with the correct simple past form of the verbs in parentheses.**

The entrepreneur Anita Roddick ____was____ born in
　　　　　　　　　　　　　　　　　1. (be)
England in 1942. She _____ the first Body
　　　　　　　　　2. (open)
Shop in 1976 in Brighton. She _____
　　　　　　　　　　　　3. (not have)
experience running a cosmetic shop, but she

_____ a lot of good ideas. She _____
4. (have)　　　　　　　　　　　　5. (want)
to "make profits with principles." For example, she _____
　　　　　　　　　　　　　　　　　6. (not allow)
her cosmetics to be tested on animals. She _____ a fair salary to
　　　　　　　　　　　　　　　　7. (pay)
all her employees.

By 1993, Anita Roddick _____ one of the five richest women in the
　　　　　　　　　　　8. (be)
world. But her principles still _____ important to her. In 2000, she
　　　　　　　　　　　　9. (remain)
_____ the world of business and _____ a full-time campaigner
10. (leave)　　　　　　　　　　　11. (become)
on social issues.

Pronunciation

4 🎧 **Listen to the sentences. Notice the pronunciation of the simple past tense verbs. Check (✓) the verbs in which** *-ed* **is pronounced as an extra syllable.**

lived	wanted ✓	loved	studied	decided	worked
acted	finished	started	watched	used	collected

5 🎧 **Listen to the verbs in Exercise 4. Then listen and repeat.**

6 **Complete the rule.**

The *-ed* ending is pronounced as an extra syllable after the sounds ____ and ____.

Speaking

7 *BEFORE YOU SPEAK.* **Make a timeline of the important dates in your life. Include dates but no other information.**

8 *PAIRS.* **Look at your partner's timeline. Take turns. Ask questions to guess the missing information.**

A: Did you get a new job in 2003?
B: No, I met my fiancé in 2003.

9 **Tell the class something interesting about your partner.**

Sabrina met her fiancé in 2003.

Writing

10 **Oprah Winfrey encourages people to share their life stories on her TV show. What story can you share? Write a paragraph about an important time or event in your life. Use regular and irregular verbs in the simple past.**

CONVERSATION TO GO

A: When **did** you **finish** school?
B: In 2002. Then I **got** a job and **bought** a new car.

13

Travel with English

Vocabulary Countries and continents; travel
Grammar *be going to* for future
Speaking Talking about plans

Getting started

1 Write the countries under the continents. Then add two more countries under Africa, Europe, Asia, and North America.

| ~~Australia~~ | Canada | India | Ireland | South Africa |

Australia	**Africa**	**Europe**	**Asia**	**North America**
Australia	_____	_____	_____	_____
	_____	_____	_____	_____
	_____	_____	_____	_____

Pronunciation

2 🎧 Listen to the names of some countries and continents. Notice the number of syllables and the stress. Write each name in the correct stress group.

○ ○	○ ○ ○	○ ○ ○
England	Italy	Korea

3 🎧 Listen and check your answers. Listen again and repeat.

4 *PAIRS.* Test your partner. Say the name of a country. Your partner says the continent it's in.

A: *Australia.*
B: *Australia.*

Reading

5 Match the words to the photos. Write the name of the country.

coast _Australia_   countryside _____   market _____

safari _____   mountains _____

6 **Read the article. Then complete the chart.**

Country	When to visit	What to see and do
Canada	November	
Australia		Sightsee in Sydney Rent a car and drive up . . .
India		
South Africa		
Ireland		

THE TRAVEL WRITER'S

Dream
Vacation

I have five months to travel before I write! I'm going to explore countries where I can practice speaking English. Where am I going to start?

Canada
It's the Rockies for me in November! There are mountains and beautiful lakes everywhere, so the views are great. I'd like to visit Nunavut, the home of the Inuit in the north of Canada, but unfortunately I'm not going to get there . . . there isn't enough time.

Australia
Australia is very hot from November to March. I love hot weather, so I'm going to arrive in Sydney in December. I'm going to sightsee in Sydney—there are so many interesting buildings in the city. Then I'm going to rent a car and drive up the coast.

India
Rajasthan is the perfect introduction to India with its festivals and monuments. There are also exciting markets to visit, with beautiful clothes and jewelry. I'm going to spend the month of January there. They say the weather is really nice then.

South Africa
South Africa offers luxury safaris and the chance to see wild animals. It also has a wonderful coastline, so, after the safari, I'm going to find a beach and go swimming there. I like the sun, so I'm going to go in February.

Ireland
In March I'm going to take part in the St. Patrick's Day festivities in Ireland. I know Ireland can be cold in the spring, but I'm going to buy a beautiful Irish sweater there. Dublin is a great city and the countryside is beautiful, so I think March is going to be a lot of fun.

Grammar focus

1 **Study the examples of *be going to* for the future.**

> **(+)** I**'m going to spend** a month in India.
> **(–)** She **isn't going to visit** the Inuit communities in Canada.
> **(?)** **Are** you **going to arrive** in December?
> (Yes, I **am**. / No, I**'m not**.)

2 **Look at the examples again. Complete the rule in the chart.**

> **be going to for future**
>
> Use a form of the verb ____ + *going to* + the base form of the verb to talk about future plans.

Grammar Reference page 143

3 **Complete the sentences with the correct form of *be going to* and the verbs in parentheses.**

1. She _isn't going to travel_ (**not travel**) to Australia in July when the weather is cold.

2. She _____ (**see**) beautiful monuments in India.

3. We _____ (**walk**) by the lake in Canada.

4. They _____ (**not stay**) in luxury hotels in India.

5. _____ (**we / swim**) in the ocean in South Africa?

6. I _____ (**visit**) Alice Springs and other famous places in Australia.

7. He _____ (**take part**) in the St. Patrick's Day festivities in Ireland.

8. _____ (**you / climb**) any mountains in Canada?

9. When _____ (**he / leave**) Rio de Janeiro?

4 **Answer these questions about the travel writer in the article on page 15.**

1. What is the woman going to do for five months?
2. Is she going to visit Nunavut in Canada? Why?
3. When is she going to arrive in Sydney? Why?
4. What is she going to do in Rajasthan?
5. Where is she going to go in February? Why?
6. What is she going to buy in Ireland?

Speaking

5 **BEFORE YOU SPEAK.** You're going to plan a group vacation to three countries where you can use your English. Look again at the article on page 15 and answer these questions. Write notes in the chart.

1. Which three countries do you want to visit?
2. When do you want to go? Why?
3. What are you going to see and do?

Place	When to visit / Why?	What to see and do
Australia	May—it's cool then	Sightsee in Sydney . . .

6 **GROUPS OF 4.** Take turns telling each other about your choices. Give reasons.

I want to go to . . . in . . . because . . .

7 Discuss your choices. Make a decision together. Where will you go? When will you go? What are you going to see and do there?

8 Tell the class your group's decisions. Can you agree on a class vacation?

Writing

9 Write a letter to a friend. Tell him or her about a trip you are planning. Where are you going to go? What are you going to do there? Use *be going to*.

CONVERSATION TO GO

A: What **are** you **going to do** next summer?
B: **I'm going to fly** around the world.

Unit 1 It's the weekend!

1 🎧 Listen to the model conversation.

2 Walk around the room. Find someone who . . .

always goes to the gym on weekends.   _____

usually goes out to eat on weekends.   _____

sometimes goes to the movies on weekends.   _____

never sleeps late on weekends.   _____

3 *PAIRS.* Compare your answers. Did you find the same people?

Unit 2 Excuses, excuses

4 🎧 Listen to the model conversation.

5 *TWO PAIRS.* Play the Health Game. Take turns. Toss a coin (one side = move ahead one space, the other side = move ahead two spaces).

When you land on a space, look at the picture. Role-play a conversation between a boss and an employee. Student A, you're the employee. You can't go to work. Give an excuse using the situation in the picture. Student B, you're the boss. Respond to the excuse. The first team to reach FINISH wins.

Unit 3 A life of achievement

6 🎧 Listen to the model conversation.

7 Write three true statements about your past. Then write three statements that are not true but sound possible.

8 *GROUPS OF 3.* Take turns. Say one statement aloud. The others in the group guess "True" or "False." After everyone guesses, tell the truth! Players receive one point for each correct guess. The person with the most points is the winner.

Points: _____

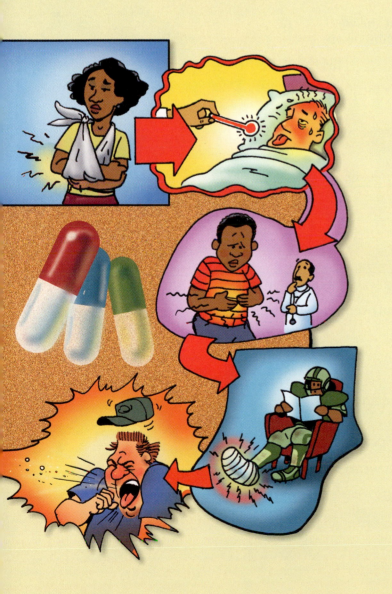

Unit 4 Travel with English

9 🎧 Listen to the model conversation.

10 *GROUPS OF 3.* Dario is going on a trip. Take turns. Ask questions to fill in his schedule. (Don't look at your partners' schedules.)

Student A, look at page 136.
Student B, look at page 138.
Student C, look at page 142.

11 *GROUPS OF 3.* Compare your schedules. Does everyone have the same information?

World of Music *1*

River Deep, Mountain High
Ike and Tina Turner

Getting Started

1 **Complete the sentences with the correct word or words.**

deep	faithful	flows	~~followed~~	goes on
let	lost	owned	puppy	robin

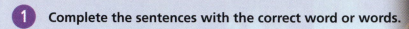

1. Tom's little sister always _followed_ him around when they were kids.

2. Ines promised to help Ralph move, but she went dancing instead. She really _____ him down.

3. Yasuhiro is really upset because he _____ his keys.

4. They're excited about their new car. It's the first one they've ever _____.

5. The river _____ into the sea a few miles from here.

6. This isn't the last stop. The train _____ to Washington.

7. The children can't wait to get home from school so they can play with their _____.

8. You know it's spring when you see a _____.

9. A _____ friend is someone who is always there to help you.

10. Don't let the children play near the pool over there. The water is very _____.

The 60s

Tina Turner was a teenager when she began singing with her husband Ike's band in the 60s. She went on to become an international superstar—and a symbol of the independent woman.

Listening

2 🎧 **Listen to the song "River Deep, Mountain High." Correct the statements.**

1. The singer is singing about a love in the past.

2. The singer thinks that her love is getting weaker.

3. The singer will be as friendly as a puppy.

3 🎧 Listen to the song again. Complete the lyrics with the words you hear.

River Deep, Mountain High

When I was a little girl I had a rag doll;
The only doll I've ever owned.
Now I love you just the way I loved that rag doll;
But only now my love has grown.
And it gets _____ in every way,
And it gets _____ let me say,
And it gets _____ day by day.

[Chorus]

Do I love you? My, oh, my!
River deep, mountain high
If I lost you, would I cry?
Oh, how I love you, baby, baby, baby, baby.

When you were a young boy did you have a puppy
that always followed you around?
Well, I'm gonna be as faithful as that puppy.
No, I'll never let you down.
'Cause it goes on and on like a river flows.
And it gets _____, baby, and heaven knows,
And it gets _____, baby, as it grows.

[Repeat chorus]

I love you, baby, like a flower loves the spring.
And I love you, baby, like a robin loves to sing.
And I love you, baby, like a schoolboy loves his pie.
And I love you, baby, river deep, mountain high.

[Repeat chorus]

4 *PAIRS.* Compare your answers.

Speaking

5 *PAIRS.* In the song "River Deep, Mountain High," what are some words that the singer uses to talk about her love?

6 *GROUPS OF 3.* Discuss the questions.

Do you like this song?
How does the song make you feel?

Culture shock

Vocabulary Social etiquette
Grammar Modals: *should* and *shouldn't* for advice
Speaking Giving advice

Lesson A

Getting started

1 Match the words and phrases in the box with the pictures. Some pictures have more than one description.

1. give a gift __D__

2. use first names ____

3. take your shoes off ____

4. shake hands ____

5. kiss ____

6. wear a suit ____

7. bow ____

8. arrive on time ____

2 *PAIRS.* **Talk about the pictures.**

Which of these things do you do in your country?

Listening

3 🎧 **Listen to a businesswoman give advice to her colleagues on living and working in the U.S. Number the topics in the order she talks about them.**

_1_ arriving for meetings

___ shaking hands

___ exchanging business cards

___ visiting someone's home

___ using a person's first or last name

___ deciding what clothing to wear

4 🎧 **Listen again and complete the statements about business etiquette in the U.S.**

1. For business appointments, always arrive _on time_____.

2. The first thing people do at meetings is _____.

3. People usually exchange _____ at some point during a meeting.

4. If it's not clear what you should call a person, use his or her _____.

5. Take flowers or a _____ when you visit someone's home.

6. Don't _____ when you enter someone's home.

7. Wear _____ to formal business meetings.

Grammar focus

1 Study the examples of *should* and *shouldn't* for advice.

> You **should arrive** on time.   You **shouldn't take** your shoes off.
> **Should** we **bow**?   Yes, you **should**. / No, you **shouldn't**.

2 Look at the examples again. Complete the rules in the chart.

should and *shouldn't* for advice
Use _____ + the base form of the verb to say that something is a good idea.
Use _____ + the base form of the verb to say that something is a bad idea.

> *Grammar Reference page 144*

3 Complete the sentences in the quiz with *should* or *shouldn't*.

Culture Quiz

1 Should you talk about business at a meal in China?
a. Yes, you __should__ . b. No, you shouldn't.

2 Should you wear a suit and tie to meet a new client in Saudi Arabia?
a. Yes, you should.   b. No, you _____ .

3 _____ you give a Brazilian purple flowers?
a. Yes, you _____. It's lucky.
b. No, you shouldn't. It's unlucky.

4 When someone gives you a gift in Japan, _____ you open it . . .
a. immediately?   b. later?

5 In Mexico, _____ you shake hands with both men and women?
a. Yes, you should.   b. No, you _____.

6 _____ you use your right hand or your left hand to accept a gift in Muslim countries?
a. right   b. left

7 In the U.S., it is important to arrive on time. When you are invited to a friend's house, you _____ arrive more than 15 minutes late.
a. true   b. false

8 You _____ touch a person on the head because it is not polite. This statement is true in which country?
a. Thailand   b. Peru

9 You _____ have a meeting in Room 4 because it is unlucky. This statement is true in which country?
a. Mexico   b. China

10 In Japan, you _____ use your boss's first name because it is not polite.
a. true   b. false

Culture Quiz answers
1.b, 2.a, 3.b, 4.b, 5.a, 6.a, 7.a, 8.a, 9.b, 10.a

4 Take the quiz. Then check your answers.

Pronunciation

5 🎧 **Listen. Notice the weak and strong pronunciations of *should* and the strong pronunciation of *shouldn't*.**

You should arrive on time.   You **shouldn't** take your shoes off.
Should I take a gift?   Yes, you **should**.
Shouldn't I wear a suit?   No, you **shouldn't**.

6 🎧 **Listen again and repeat.**

7 🎧 **Listen and underline the word you hear.**

1. You **should** / **shouldn't** arrive early.
2. You **should** / **shouldn't** ask questions.
3. **Should** / **Shouldn't** I use first names?
4. You **should** / **shouldn't** take flowers.
5. **Should** / **Shouldn't** I shake hands with everyone?

Speaking

8 ***BEFORE YOU SPEAK.*** **Some friends from another country are going to visit your country. What should they do while visiting? What shouldn't they do? Write your ideas about the topics.**

9 ***GROUPS OF 4.*** **Compare the advice you're going to give your friends. What advice is the same? What advice is different?**

Greeting/Saying hello
 You should . . .
 You shouldn't . . .
Giving gifts

Eating

Clothes

Other

Writing

10 **Write an email to a friend who is going to visit your country. Give advice about what he or she should and shouldn't do during the trip.**

CONVERSATION TO GO

A: **Should** I bow when I meet someone?
B: No, you **shouldn't**. You **should** shake hands.

Party time!

Vocabulary Planning parties
Grammar Expressions for making suggestions
Speaking Making suggestions

Getting started

1 *PAIRS.* **Look at the photos. In which photo can you see . . .**

1. a birthday party? ___
2. a costume party? ___
3. a going-away party? ___

2 *PAIRS.* **Discuss the questions.**

Do you like parties?

What is your favorite kind of party?

Have you ever been to a going-away party or a costume party?

How do you usually celebrate your birthday?

3 Complete the pairs of sentences with words from the box.

| afford | buy | ~~cost~~ | pay | rent | spend |

1. A birthday cake can ___cost___ about $25.
   The gifts for Sue and Ron's going-away party ___cost___ a lot.

2. I'm going to _____ a new dress for the party.
   I want to _____ a gift for you.

3. Can you _____ that suit? It's very expensive.
   I can't _____ a fancy restaurant. I don't have much money.

4. John is going to _____ for dinner on your birthday.
   He'll _____ by credit card.

5. I usually _____ a lot of money on birthday cards.
   We're going to _____ $300 on the party.

6. I want to _____ a car for the weekend.
   He's going to _____ a ballroom at a hotel for the party.

4 *PAIRS.* Take turns saying three sentences about yourself or people you know. Use the verbs from Exercise 3.

Listening

5 🎧 Listen to a professional party planner talking with a client from an advertising company. They are discussing the company's yearly office party. Check (✓) the things they talk about.

Party Planners, Etc.

- ○ date of the party
- ✓ place
- ○ gifts
- ○ number of guests
- ○ music
- ○ food
- ○ parking

6 🎧 Listen again and underline the correct information.

1. The party is going to be at **a hotel** / **the office**.
2. They're going to have **a band** / **a DJ**.
3. They're going to serve **dessert** / **dinner**.

Grammar focus

1 **Study the examples. Notice the ways to make suggestions.**

> **How about** looking at how much we spent last year?
> **Why don't** we rent the room at the Sheraton again?
> **Let's (not)** have it at the office.
> **Maybe** you **could** get a DJ this time.

2 **Look at the examples again. Complete the rules in the chart.**

Why don't/How about/Let's (not)/Maybe . . . could for suggestions
Use _____ + verb + *-ing*.
Use _____ + subject + *could* + the base form of the verb.
Use _____ + subject + the base form of the verb.
Use _____ + the base form of the verb.

> **Grammar Reference page 144**

3 **Complete the conversation with the expressions in the box.**

Why don't   How about   Let's (not)   Maybe . . . could

A: **(1)** _____Let's_____ have a party next weekend!

B: Good idea. **(2)** _____ getting a band?

A: I don't know. That's expensive. **(3)** _____ we get a DJ instead?

B: But my brother is in a band. **(4)** _____ we _____
 ask them to play for free?

A: OK. Now, what about the food? **(5)** _____ cooking something?

B: Cooking? That's too much work! **(6)** _____ just have
 sandwiches and chips.

A: **(7)** _____ we _____ have cheese and crackers, too.

B: That sounds fine, but **(8)** _____ spend too much money on food.

A: Right. **(9)** _____ you buy the food? **(10)**_____ you

 (11) _____ get everything at SuperSavers. It's cheaper there.

Pronunciation

4 🎧 **Listen. Notice the way the focus word (the most important word) in each sentence stands out from the other words.**

A: Let's have a **par**ty next weekend.

B: Good i**de**a. Why don't we get a **band**?

A: We can't af**ford** it. How about getting a **D**J?

B: **O**K. What about **food**?

A: Maybe we could order **piz**za.

B: I don't **like** pizza. Why don't we just have **snacks**?

5 🎧 **Listen again and repeat.**

Speaking

6 *GROUPS OF 4.* **Your group is going to work together to plan a party. First, choose the purpose of the party.**

- Surprise birthday party for (name)
- End-of-the-year party
- Other: _____

Now think about your budget. You have $500. Look at the costs on page 140. Make suggestions. Decide together how you will spend the money.

A: *Let's have the party at a hotel.*
B: *Why don't we have it at the office? We can save $150.*

7 **Tell the class about your group's party plans.**

Writing

8 **You are a party planner for a company called Parties Unlimited. People write to you for advice on giving parties. Read the email messages on page 136 and write replies to each one. Use *maybe you could*, *why don't you*, and *how about*.**

CONVERSATION TO GO

A: It's your birthday. **Let's** have a party!
B: I'd rather get a gift!

Lesson A

First impressions

Vocabulary Words to describe physical appearance
Grammar *be* and *have* with descriptions
Speaking Describing people

Getting started

1 Write the descriptions in the box next to the correct words in the word webs.

average height	average weight	bald	beard	curly
elderly	heavy	middle-aged	mustache	short
sideburns	slim	straight	tall	~~young~~

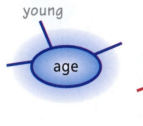

young

age

weight

height

hair

2 *PAIRS.* **Look at the photos. Take turns using the words from Exercise 1 to describe someone in the pictures. Your partner guesses which person you are describing.**

A: *Tall and slim.*
B: *Picture A.*
A: *Yes!*

A   B

Listening

3 🎧 Listen to the conversation between two women. They're talking about two friends, Maurice and Julia. Check (✓) the pictures of Maurice and Julia.

Maurice

a. ☐   b. ☐

Julia

a. ☐   b. ☐

4 🎧 Listen again and circle the letter of the correct answer.

1. Maurice and Amy know each other because they ____.
   a. work in the same office
   b. are in the same English class
   c. met at a party

2. Maurice wants Cristina's phone number because he wants to ____.
   a. study English with her
   b. ask her on a date
   c. have coffee with her

3. Amy ____ give Cristina's phone number to Maurice.
   a. is going to
   b. isn't going to
   c. can't

31

Grammar focus

1 **Study the examples of *be* and *have* for descriptions.**

> He**'s** in his 20s, probably about 28.
> She**'s** average height.
> He**'s** quite slim.
>
> She **has** long, straight hair.
> He **has** hazel eyes.
> He **doesn't have** a mustache or beard.

2 **Look at the examples again. Circle the correct verb to complete the rules in the chart.**

be/have with descriptions
Use ***be / have*** to talk about a person's age, height, and weight.
Use ***be / have*** to talk about a person's hair and eyes.
Note the following exception: *He **is** bald*.

> *Grammar Reference page 144*

3 **Complete the descriptions with the correct forms of *be* or *have*.
You can use contractions.**

My friend Judy and I **(1)** ____are____ both 21 years old,

but she and I look completely different. I **(2)** _____

short, and she **(3)** _____ tall. I **(4)** _____ a little

heavy, and she **(5)** _____ average weight.

I **(6)** _____ long, curly blond hair, and she

(7) _____ long, straight black hair.

My friends Tony and Tom are identical twins. They look

exactly alike. They **(8)** _____ about 30. They

(9) _____ black hair and brown eyes. They

(10) _____ tall, and they **(11)** _____ slim.

 The only way I can tell them apart is this:

Tony **(12)** _____ a mustache, and Tom

(13) _____ (not) one.

Pronunciation

4 🎧 **Listen. Notice the weak pronunciations of *and* and *or*.**

She's tall and slim.
He's average height and has black hair.
He has curly brown hair and hazel eyes.
She has long black hair and brown eyes.

I'm not tall or slim.
He isn't short or heavy.
He doesn't have a beard or mustache.
She doesn't have blond hair or blue eyes.

5 🎧 **Listen again and repeat.**

Speaking

6 *PAIRS.* **You're going to the airport to meet your partner's visitors. Take turns describing the people and finding them in the picture.**

Student A, look at page 137. Student B, look at the picture on the left. Find each person that your partner describes. Did you find the right person? Check with your partner.

A: My colleague, Sandra Vazquez, is going to arrive on Saturday. Can you meet her at the airport?

B: Sure. What does she look like?

A: She . . .

7 **Now switch roles. Student B, look at page 139.**

Writing

8 Write a paragraph describing someone's physical appearance. Write about a family member, a friend, or a famous person. Use *be* and *have*.

CONVERSATION TO GO

A: What does she look like?
B: She**'s tall** and **slim**. She **has curly brown hair** and **brown eyes**.

UNIT 8

At the movies

Vocabulary Words related to the movies
Grammar *say* and *tell*
Speaking Talking about movies

Lesson A

A

B

Getting started

1 Match the quotes with the photos.

1. ____ "The best romantic movie in the history of film. A classic black-and-white movie."

2. ____ "Another fast and exciting action movie."

3. ____ "Best science fiction film ever."

4. ____ "It makes everyone laugh. A comedy for the entire family."

2 In which photo(s) can you see . . .

1. an actor? _____

2. an actress? _____

3. special effects? _____

4. costumes? _____

C

3 **PAIRS.** Discuss the questions.

What kinds of movies do you like?
Who is your favorite actor or actress?
What movies are playing now in movie theaters?
Which ones do you want to see? Why?

D

Reading

4 Read the article about memorable moments in film history. Then circle the letter of the correct answer.

1. Which movie does Tomás like?
   (a.) *Star Wars*   b. *Casablanca*
2. Why does he like it?
   a. the actors   b. the special effects
3. Which movie does Reiko like?
   a. *Star Wars*   b. *Dr. No*
4. Why does she like it?
   a. the scenery   b. the actor
5. Which movie does Mariana like?
   a. *Dr. No*   b. *Casablanca*
6. Why does she like it?
   a. the story   b. the director

"In your opinion, what are the most memorable movies in the history of film?" That's the question we asked our readers.

"I think the first *Star Wars* movie is the best science fiction film. I didn't like the new ones very much, but the original *Star Wars* is a fantastic movie. The special effects are amazing, and the story is interesting. I can't remember the names of the actors, but I love the scene where Luke fights Darth Vader." **Tomás, Mexico**

"I love James Bond movies, and my favorite is *Dr. No.* It was the first 007 movie, and although the beginning is slow, the ending is excellent. Sean Connery was the best actor who played James Bond, and he always will be." **Reiko, Japan**

"One of my favorite movies is *Casablanca*—I love old, romantic films. I think the story and the music are really good. Black-and-white films are my favorites." **Mariana, Brazil**

5 Read the article again and check (✓) the adjective(s) used to describe things about each movie.

	Star Wars	Dr. No	Casablanca
amazing			
excellent			
fantastic	✓		
good			
interesting			
romantic			
slow			

8

Grammar focus

1 Study the examples with *say* and *tell*. Underline the object.

> Tomás **said** (that) he **really** liked *Star Wars*.
> He **told us** (that) he **loved** the special effects.
> Mariana **told me** (that) she **loved** *Casablanca*.
> She **said** (that) black-and-white films **were** her favorites.

2 Look at the examples again. Circle the correct word to complete the rules in the chart.

say and *tell*
There is no object after **say / tell**.
There is always an object after **say / tell**.
Use the ***present / past*** after *said* and *told*.
NOTE: You can leave out the word ***that*** after **say** and **tell**.

 Grammar Reference page 144

3 Circle *said* or *told* in each sentence.

1. She **said** / **told** she liked comedies.
2. He **said** / **told** me he went to the movies every weekend.
3. I **said** / **told** that I didn't go to the movies very often.
4. Tara **said** / **told** Elizabeth that she loved science fiction films.
5. Elizabeth **said** / **told** that she hated action movies.
6. I **said** / **told** Carlos that I was taking a filmmaking course.
7. Carlos **said** / **told** me he didn't want to take the course.
8. Pete **said** / **told** he was late for the movies.
9. Rachel **said** / **told** that he had to hurry.
10. He **said** / **told** me his favorite actress was Halle Berry.

4 Complete the sentences. Use the correct form of *say* or *tell* and the correct form of the verb in parentheses.

1. Tomás _____told_____ John that the special effects in *Star Wars* _____were_____ (be) amazing.

2. Reiko _____ that she _____ (love) James Bond films.

3. She _____ me that Sean Connery _____ (be) a good actor.

4. She _____ that *Dr. No* _____ (be) her favorite Bond movie.

5. Mariana _____ her favorite film _____ (be) *Casablanca*.

6. She _____ us that she _____ (like) old films.

7. She _____ me that she _____ (love) the music in *Casablanca*.

Pronunciation

5 🎧 **Listen. Notice the groups of consonant sounds in the words.**

a **cl**assic **bl**ack-and-white fi**lm**   the be**st** scie**nce** fi**cti**on movie

an int**er**esting **st**ory   a **sl**ow **st**art

exci**t**ing **sp**ecial effe**cts**   an excelle**nt** a**ctr**ess

He said that he li**ked** *Star Wars*.   She to**ld** us she lov**ed** old fi**lms**.

6 🎧 **Listen again and repeat.**

Speaking

7 **BEFORE YOU SPEAK.** **Make notes about your favorite movie.**

8 **PAIRS.** **Take turns asking each other questions and telling about your favorite movie. Use your notes.**

A: *My favorite movie is a classic—*
E.T. It's a science fiction movie.
I loved the story.

B: *Who are the actors?*

9 **Tell the class what you learned about your partner's favorite movie.**

Elena's favorite movie is E.T.
She said that she loved the story.

> Name of film:
>
> Actor(s)/Actress(es):
>
> Director:
>
> Story:
>
> Special effects:
>
> Music:
>
> Scenery:
>
> Costumes:

Writing

10 **Write a short review of a good movie you recently saw. Include information about the actors, director, story, special effects, music, scenery, and costumes.**

CONVERSATION TO GO

A: Steve **said** he **liked** Bond movies because of the special effects.
B: Really? He **told me** he **liked** Bond movies because of the beautiful actresses!

Unit 5 Culture shock

1 🎧 Look at the list of situations. Then listen to the model conversation.

- meet a friend's parents for the first time
- pick someone up at the airport
- go to class on the first day
- go to dinner with your boss
- start a new job
- go to a job interview
- go to a friend's home for dinner
- go to a surprise birthday party

2 Choose a situation from the list in Exercise 1, but don't say it aloud. Think about the things you should and shouldn't do in that situation.

3 *GROUPS OF 4.* Play the guessing game. Take turns. Say what you should and shouldn't do in the situation you chose. Your partner will guess the situation.

Unit 6 Party time!

4 *GROUPS OF 3.* You planned a party together. Now the party is over. Look at the picture. This is the scene before the people arrived. Describe the scene.

5 🎧 Imagine that it is now last week and you are just starting to plan the party. Listen to the model conversation.

6 Role-play. Pretend that you're planning the party. You want the party to look like the picture. Take turns. Make suggestions for planning the party.

Unit 7 First impressions

7 🎧 Listen to the model conversation.

8 *PAIRS.* Student A, go to page 137. Student B, go to page 139. Look at the pictures. Take turns describing the person in each one. How many people are the same?

Unit 8 At the movies

9 🎧 Listen to the model conversation.

10 Interview five people. Find out what kind of movies they like. Take notes in the chart.

Name	Favorite kind of movie	Favorite movie	Why?

11 Report back to the class about your classmates' favorite movies.

What would you like?

Vocabulary Words related to eating at a restaurant
Grammar *would like/like, would prefer/prefer*
Speaking Ordering food and drinks in a restaurant

Getting started

1 *GROUPS OF 3.* **Look at the words in the box. Find them in the photos.**

customer	fork	glass	knife	menu
napkin	pepper	salt	spoon	waiter

The Shrimp Boat

APPETIZERS

Shrimp Cocktail
Soup of the Day
Garden Salad

* * *

ENTRÉES

Shrimp Savoy
Shrimp Plaza
Shrimp Ritz

served with rice or pasta
and mixed vegetables

* * *

DESSERTS

Cheesecake
Chocolate Ice Cream
Raspberry Sorbet
Coffee   Tea
Cappuccino   Espresso

2 Look at the menu. Complete the sentences with the words in the box.

~~appetizer~~	dessert	entrée
side dish	tea	

1. The soup is an ___appetizer___ .
2. The Shrimp Savoy is an _____.
3. The pasta is a _____.
4. The ice cream is a _____.
5. After your meal, you can have coffee or _____.

3 *PAIRS.* Discuss the questions.

How often do you go to restaurants?
What is your favorite restaurant?
Why do you like it?

Listening

4 🎧 Look at the menu. Listen to two people ordering a meal at The Shrimp Boat. On the menu, put an *M* next to the food the man orders and a *W* next to the food the woman orders.

5 🎧 Listen again. Match the name of the dish with the description.

1. Shrimp Savoy ____

   a. shrimp in black olive sauce with tomatoes and herbs

2. Shrimp Plaza ____

   b. shrimp in tomato sauce with herbs and olives

3. Shrimp Ritz ____

   c. shrimp in herb sauce with tomatoes and olives

Grammar focus

1 **Look at the examples. Write *a* or *b* in each blank.**

> Key: a = what you like in general
>   b = what you want now or in the future

1. **Do** you **prefer** chocolate ice cream or vanilla ice cream?
   I **prefer** chocolate. __a__

2. **Do** you **like** seafood?
   Yes, I **do**. I **like** all kinds of seafood. _____

3. **Would** you **prefer** rice or pasta?
   I**'d prefer** the rice. _____

4. What **would** you **like**?
   I**'d like** the Shrimp Savoy. _____

2 **Look at the examples again. Circle *a* or *b* to complete the rules in the chart.**

would like/like, would prefer/prefer
Use _____ to talk about things you like in general.
a. *I like* or *I prefer*   b. *I'd like* or *I'd prefer*
Use _____ to ask for something you want.
a. *I like* or *I prefer*   b. *I'd like* or *I'd prefer*
NOTE: *I'd prefer = I would prefer; I'd like = I would like*

Grammar Reference page 145

3 **Circle the correct answers.**

1. A: Would you like a table near the window?
   B: Yes, I like to sit near the window. / Yes, thank you.
2. A: Do you prefer black or green olives?
   B: I'd prefer black. / I prefer black.
3. A: Would you like to see the menu?
   B: Yes, we would, thanks. / We like the menu.
4. A: Would you prefer soup or salad?
   B: I prefer soup. / I'd prefer soup.

Pronunciation

4 🎧 Listen to the weak and strong pronunciations of *would*. Notice the /d/ sound in *I'd like* and *I'd prefer* and the linking in *would you*.

What would you like?   I'**d** like the shrimp.

Would you like salad?   Yes, thanks. I **would**.

Would you prefer rice or pasta?   I'**d** prefer pasta.

5 🎧 Listen again and repeat.

Speaking

6 *PAIRS.* Use the cues to complete the conversation between a waiter and a customer.

Waiter:	*Order?* Would you like to order?	**Waiter:**	*Dessert?*
Customer:	*The shrimp.*	**Customer:**	*Yes.*
Waiter:	*An appetizer?*	**Waiter:**	*Cake or ice cream?*
Customer:	*No.*	**Customer:**	*Cake.*
Waiter:	*Drink?*	**Waiter:**	*Anything else?*
Customer:	*Iced tea.*	**Customer:**	*Check, please.*

7 *GROUPS OF 3.* Student A, you are a waiter/waitress at Rosie's Restaurant. Students B and C, you are customers. Student A, look at this page. Students B and C, look at page 142. Student A, take the customers' order. Write it on the guest check.

Writing

8 You're a famous chef. You're going to open a new American restaurant in your city. What would you like to have on the menu? Write a memo to the person who will design the menu. Include information about appetizers, entrées, side dishes, desserts, and drinks.

CONVERSATION TO GO

A: **Would** you **like** the check?
B: No, thank you!

Lesson A

Big issues

Getting started

1 **Match the words on the left with the examples on the right.**

1. economy _b_
2. transportation ___
3. space ___
4. politics ___
5. population ___
6. communication ___
7. climate ___

a. United States: 288 million people
b. money, bank
c. rainy, hot
d. car, airplane, bus
e. the moon, Mars, a space station
f. phone, fax, email
g. government, president, the White House

Pronunciation

2 🎧 **Listen. Notice the stressed (strong) syllable in each word. Mark the stress.**

• climate	prediction
transportation	politics
population	communication
economy	government

3 🎧 **Listen again and repeat. Check your answers.**

4 *PAIRS.* **Look at the photos. Tell which photo matches each topic in Exercise 1.**

I think Photo A matches politics.

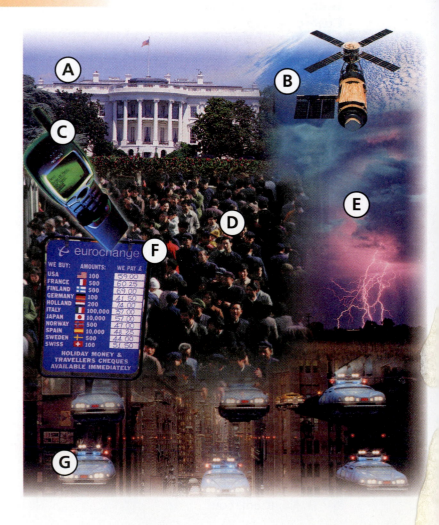

Reading

5 Arthur C. Clarke is a scientist. He has also written many science fiction novels, including *2001: A Space Odyssey*. Read his predictions.

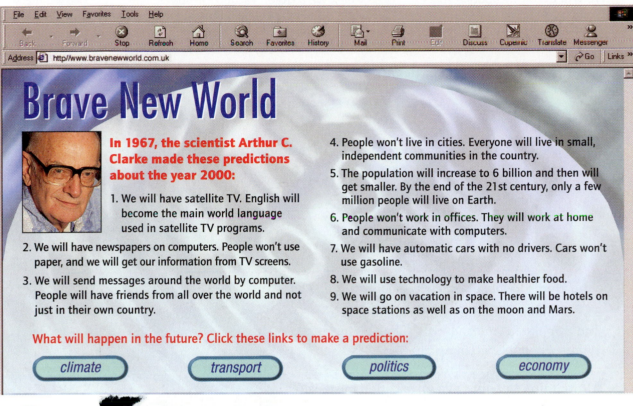

Brave New World

In 1967, the scientist Arthur C. Clarke made these predictions about the year 2000:

1. We will have satellite TV. English will become the main world language used in satellite TV programs.

2. We will have newspapers on computers. People won't use paper, and we will get our information from TV screens.

3. We will send messages around the world by computer. People will have friends from all over the world and not just in their own country.

4. People won't live in cities. Everyone will live in small, independent communities in the country.

5. The population will increase to 6 billion and then will get smaller. By the end of the 21st century, only a few million people will live on Earth.

6. People won't work in offices. They will work at home and communicate with computers.

7. We will have automatic cars with no drivers. Cars won't use gasoline.

8. We will use technology to make healthier food.

9. We will go on vacation in space. There will be hotels on space stations as well as on the moon and Mars.

What will happen in the future? Click these links to make a prediction:

(climate)   (transport)   (politics)   (economy)

6 *PAIRS.* Which of Arthur C. Clarke's predictions have come true? Put a check (✓) next to the predictions that are true for most people today.

7 Complete the predictions from the reading with the words in the box.

cars	space	~~programs~~	messages	offices
cities	food	the news	population	

1. We will have satellite TV _programs_.

2. We will read _____ on the computer.

3. People around the world will send _____ to each other by computer.

4. No one will live in _____.

5. The _____ of the world will get smaller.

6. No one will work in _____.

7. _____ won't need drivers or gasoline.

8. The _____ we eat will be healthier.

9. There will be hotels in _____.

Grammar focus

1 **Study the examples of *will* for predicting.**

We **will go** on vacation in space.	I think we**'ll go** on vacation in space.
People **won't live** in cities.	I don't think people **will live** in cities.
What **will happen** in the future?	What do you think **will happen**?

2 **Look at the examples again. Circle the correct words to complete the rules in the chart.**

***will* for predicting**

After *will* or *won't,* use **the base form of the verb / verb + *-ing*.**

Use **I *think* + subject + won't / I don't think + subject + *will*** to predict what will not happen.

> **Grammar Reference page 145**

3 **Use the words to make sentences about the year 2100.**

1. The population of the world / not increase.
   The population of the world won't increase.
2. Where / people / go on vacation?

3. I / not think / people / go on vacation in space.

4. Everyone / have / a computer?

5. I think / everyone / speak one language.

6. The world's weather / not get warmer.

7. You think / technology / cost less?

8. I think / transportation / be cheaper.

9. The world economy / be stronger.

10. There be / flying cars.

11. I / not think / we find life on another planet.

Speaking

4 **GROUPS OF 3.** You are visiting a website called Y2K100. It asks you to send your predictions for the year 2100. Discuss your predictions for the topics below.

In 2100, people will work ten hours a week.

> politics   transportation
>
> clothing   food
>
> work   economy
>
> communication   climate
>
> vacations

5 Change groups and discuss your predictions. Are there any predictions that everyone agrees on?

Writing

6 Look again at the web page on page 45. Use Arthur C. Clarke's predictions as a model. Write your own web page with predictions about five big issues for the year 2050. Use *will*.

CONVERSATION TO GO

A: In 2050, math **will** still **be** an important subject in school.
B: I hope not!

47

Hard work

Vocabulary Activities related to work
Grammar *have to/don't have to*
Speaking Describing jobs

Getting started

1 Complete the job descriptions with the words in the boxes.

| type letters and contracts | ~~arrange meetings~~ | make decisions |

Administrative Assistant

"I work for a lawyer. My boss tells me what he needs, and I call clients to **(1)** ___arrange meetings___. I also use a computer to **(2)** _____. Sometimes I don't like my job because I can't **(3)** _____. Mostly I do what my boss tells me to do."

| meet with clients | travel | communicate | give presentations |

Sales Manager

"I sell computer software for a large company. I have clients all over the country, and I **(1)** _____ to different cities all the time. I like to **(2)** _____ because I enjoy talking to people in person. When I'm traveling, I use a laptop to **(3)** _____ about my company's products. I use my cell phone and email to **(4)** _____ with my clients and boss when I'm on the road."

| work as a team | make much money | wait on customers | work long hours |

Salesperson

"I work in a large department store. I **(1)** _____ and help them find what they are looking for. I **(2)** _____ with other salespeople in my department. We all **(3)** _____; for example, I work from 11:00 A.M. to 9:00 P.M., Tuesday through Sunday. We don't **(4)** _____, but we get employee discounts on the things we buy."

2 **GROUPS OF 3.** Talk about activities you do in your job now or want to do in a future job.

Reading

3 Look at the photo of the pizza delivery person. Which two activities in Exercise 1 do you think he does in his job?

_____   _____

4 Read the article "Nine to Five." Then check your guesses in Exercise 3.

Name: Marcus Willis

Job: Pizza delivery person

Wages: $5.50/hour

Nine to Five

So you think my job is easy? You pick up the pizza, drive around town, go back to the shop, and then do it all again. It isn't that easy.

First, I don't earn much per hour, so I have to work long hours—sometimes I start at 3:00 P.M. and finish at 2:00 A.M. I also have to drive a lot. I drive about 80 miles every day, and I have to use my own car because the company doesn't give me one. That's a real problem. Another problem is the tips. Customers don't have to give me tips, but without the extra money, I don't earn much. Finally, I'm always busy. When I finish driving, I have to wait on customers in the shop and, of course, I have to be polite, even when I'm tired! Then my boss answers the phone, and I have to leave again and deliver another pizza.

The next time a delivery person brings you a pizza, remember: Does he have to work hard? Yes, he does! So be nice to him, and give him a big tip!

5 How does Marcus feel about his job? Read the article again and write *T* (true) or *F* (false) after each statement.

Marcus feels that . . .

1. delivering pizza is a difficult job.

2. his job pays well.

3. the pizza company should give him a car.

4. getting tips is important.

5. he isn't always busy at work.

Grammar focus

1 **Study the examples with *have to*.**

> I **have to** work long hours.
> He **has to** pick up the pizza.
> **Does** he **have to** work hard? Yes, he **does**. / No, he **doesn't**.
> Customers **don't have to** give him tips.

2 **Look at the examples again. Complete the rules in the chart with *is* or *isn't*.**

have to/don't have to
Use *have to/has to* + the base form of the verb when something _____ necessary.
Use *don't have to/doesn't have to* + the base form of the verb when something _____ necessary.

> *Grammar Reference page 145*

3 **Write conversations. Use the words given and the correct form of *have to*.**

1. A: What / do / in your job? *What do you have to do in your job?*
   B: We / meet clients. *We have to meet clients.*
2. A: What / your boss / do?
   B: He / give presentations.
3. A: You / travel?
   B: Yes / do.
4. A: You / work as a team?
   B: No / not.
5. A: She / use a computer?
   B: Yes / she / answer email from customers.

Pronunciation

4 🎧 **Listen. Notice the pronunciation of *have to* ("hafta") and *has to* ("hasta").**

have to	have to work	I have to work long hours.

Does he have to work hard?

has to	has to drive	He has to drive a lot.

He has to pick up the pizza.

5 🎧 **Listen again and repeat.**

6 ***PAIRS.* Practice the conversations in Exercise 3.**

Speaking

7 **BEFORE YOU SPEAK.** Look at the list of jobs. Add one more job to the list. Complete the chart with activities people *have to* do and *don't have to* do in these jobs. Then rank the jobs in your order of preference (1 = the best and 6 = the worst).

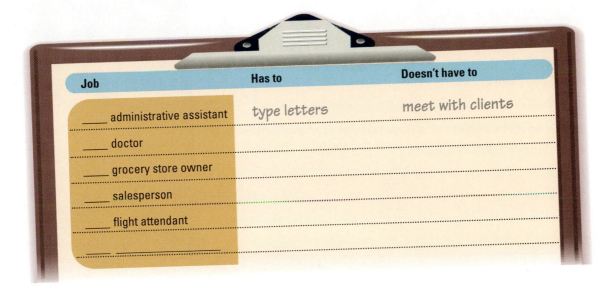

Job	Has to	Doesn't have to
_____ administrative assistant	type letters	meet with clients
_____ doctor		
_____ grocery store owner		
_____ salesperson		
_____ flight attendant		
_____ _____		

8 **GROUPS OF 3.** Which jobs do you think are best and worst. Discuss your opinions and give reasons.

A: *I think doctors have the worst job. They have to help very sick people.*
   They have to work long hours.
B: *I don't think they have the worst job. They don't have to . . .*

9 Compare your group's answers with the rest of the class. Which job did most people think was the best? The worst?

Writing

10 Imagine that you are working in your ideal job. Write an article like the one on page 49 describing a typical day at work. Describe the activities that you *have to* do and *don't have to* do every day.

CONVERSATION TO GO

A: **Do** you **have to make** decisions in your job?
B: Yes, I **do**. Umm . . . no, I **don't**. Well, yes . . .

UNIT 12

Island life

Vocabulary Practical activities
Grammar Present perfect for indefinite past: *ever, never*
Speaking Talking about practical experience

Lesson A

Getting started

1 *PAIRS.* **Look at the photo of Mulkinney Island. Would you like to live there? Why?**

2 **Read the advertisement for a new television show,** *Adventure Island*. **Complete the sentences with the verbs in the box.**

build	catch	grow	have	make
spend	take care of	~~travel~~	work	

Adventure Island

A new reality TV show

Do you like to **(1)** ___travel___ to new places and **(2)** _____ time outdoors? Are you ready to **(3)** _____ an adventure?

Mulkinney Island is in the north Atlantic. No one lives there. There are no houses, no stores, and no hospitals. We are looking for sixteen adventurous people from around the world to live on the island for a year.

We need people who can **(4)** _____ houses, **(5)** _____ clothes, and **(6)** _____ food.

We also need people who know how to **(7)** _____ fish, **(8)** _____ on a farm, and **(9)** _____ animals.

Send your application today. Explain why we should pick you to join us on Adventure Island!

3 *PAIRS.* **Compare your answers in Exercise 2.**

52

4   What other abilities will be useful on the island? Check *Yes* or *No* and write why.

Does *Adventure Island* need people who can . . .	Yes	No	Why?
use a computer?			
start a business?			
cook for a large group?			
write newspaper articles?			
teach a class?			

5   *PAIRS.* Compare your answers.

I don't think Adventure Island needs people who can use a computer. There are no computers on the island!

Reading

6   Andrew Ho wants to be on *Adventure Island*. Read his application form.
Then check (✓) *Yes* or *No* to each question about his experience.

Name: Andrew Ho

Age: 25

REALITY ADVENTURE
ADVENTURE ISLAND
TELEVISION

1. Have you ever spent time outdoors?   YES ☐   NO ☐

I've gone camping many times, and I like hiking and mountain climbing. I've also gone fishing in the ocean, and I've caught a lot of fish! I love the outdoors.

2. Have you ever worked on a farm?   YES ☐   NO ☐

I haven't worked on a farm, but my family has had several pets, and I think I'm good at taking care of animals. I've had a vegetable garden, and I've grown carrots, tomatoes, and lettuce in my backyard.

3. Have you ever lived overseas?   YES ☐   NO ☐

I've never lived overseas, but I've traveled abroad and around the United States. I like to travel and meet new people. I'm an adventurous person.

4. Have you ever cooked for large groups?   YES ☐   NO ☐

I'm a cook in a hospital. I think this experience will be useful because I cook for large groups all the time.

7   Discuss. Is Andrew Ho a good choice for *Adventure Island*? Why? What can he do?

Grammar focus

1 **Look again at the application form on page 53 and answer the questions.**

Is Andrew growing vegetables now?
Do we know exactly when he grew vegetables?

2 **Study the examples of the present perfect for the indefinite past.**

I**'ve grown** vegetables in my backyard.
My family **has had** a lot of pets.
Have you **ever spent** time outdoors? Yes, I **have**. / No, I **haven't**.
I **haven't worked** on a farm.
I**'ve never lived** overseas.

3 **Look at the examples again. Circle the correct words to complete the rules in the chart.**

Present perfect: indefinite past; *ever, never*

Use the present perfect when the exact time of an action **is / is not** important.

Use *have* or *has* + the **present / past** participle to form the present perfect.

Use **never / ever** + present perfect to ask a question.

Use *not* or **never / ever** + present perfect to make a negative statement.

NOTE: The past participle of regular verbs is the base form of the verb + *-ed*.
See page 150 for a list of irregular past participles.

Grammar Reference page 146

4 **Complete the conversations with the correct present perfect form of the verbs in parentheses.**

1. A: __Have__ they ever ___used___ (**use**) a computer?

   B: Yes, they __have__.

2. A: _____ you ever _____ (**build**) a fire?

   B: Yes, I _____. I _____ (**go**) camping several times.

3. A: _____ she ever _____ (**take care of**) farm animals?

   B: No, she _____, but she _____ (**have**) a few pets.

4. A: _____ they ever _____ (**live**) overseas?

   B: They _____ (**not live**) overseas, but they _____ (**travel**) abroad.

5. A: _____ you ever _____ (**go**) fishing?

   B: Yes, I _____. I _____ (**go**) hiking, too.

6. A: _____ he ever _____ (**cook**) for large groups?

   B: Yes, he _____. He's a cook in a hospital.

Pronunciation

5 🎧 Listen. Notice how a vowel sound at the end of a word links to a vowel sound at the beginning of the next word.

Have you^wever   Have you ever lived overseas?

Has he^yever   Has he ever grown vegetables?

Have you^wever   Have you ever spent time outdoors?

Have they^yever   Have they ever used a computer?

6 🎧 Listen and repeat.

Speaking

7 ***BEFORE YOU SPEAK.*** **Look at the chart and check (✓) the activities that you have done. Then add two more activities to the chart.**

Activities	You	Classmate 1	Classmate 2
grow vegetables			
take care of animals			
go camping			
make clothes			
catch a fish			
travel overseas			

8 ***GROUPS OF 3.*** **Interview each other. Ask follow-up questions to get more information. Record the answers in the chart.**

A: *Have you ever grown vegetables?*
B: *Yes, I have.*
A: *Really? What kind of vegetables?*
B: *I've grown tomatoes.*

9 Which person in your group should be on the TV show *Adventure Island*?

Writing

10 The TV show *Adventure Island* has invited you to apply for their next adventure. Are you ready to go? Write a letter explaining why you should go. Describe the things you have done that will help you on the island. Use the present perfect.

CONVERSATION TO GO

A: **Have you ever made** your own clothes?
B: Yes, **I have**.

Unit 9 What would you like?

1 🎧 Listen to the model conversation.

2 *PAIRS.* Make the menu for your own American restaurant. Think of a name for the restaurant. Then think of two interesting appetizers, two entrées, two side dishes, and two desserts. Write the names of the dishes in the menu. (Be sure you can describe each dish.)

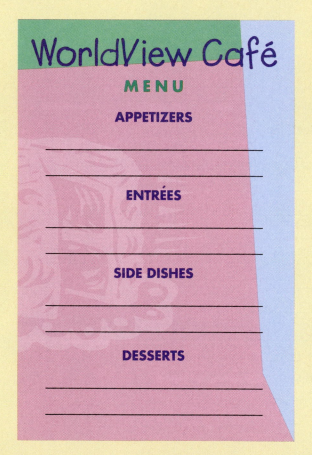

WorldView Café

MENU

APPETIZERS

_____

_____

ENTRÉES

_____

_____

SIDE DISHES

_____

_____

DESSERTS

_____

_____

3 *PAIRS.* Find a new partner. Student A, you're the waiter; Student B, you're the customer. The waiter gives the menu to the customer and explains the dishes on it. The customer orders. Then switch roles.

4 Discuss. Which restaurant has the best or the most interesting menu?

Unit 10 Big issues

5 🎧 Listen to the model conversation.

6 Make three predictions about the future. Predict something that will happen in 20 years, in 50 years, and in 100 years. Write your predictions on the timeline.

Today   20 years   50 years   100 years

7 Walk around the room. Tell one of your predictions to a classmate, and ask if he or she agrees with it. If your classmate agrees, you get one point. Continue telling classmates your predictions. The person with the most points at the end of the game is the winner.

8 Share your results with the class. Which predictions did the most people agree with? Which did they disagree with?

Unit 11 Hard work

9 🎧 Listen to the model conversation.

10 *GROUPS OF 3.* Student A, think of a job. Students B and C, ask *Yes/No* questions about the job. When you have enough information, guess what job it is. Keep track of the number of questions you ask. Take turns until everyone thinks of a job and everyone asks and answers questions. The person whose job requires the most questions wins.

Unit 12 Island life

11 🎧 Listen to the model conversation.

12 Check (✔) at least six activities that you have done. (You can use your imagination.)

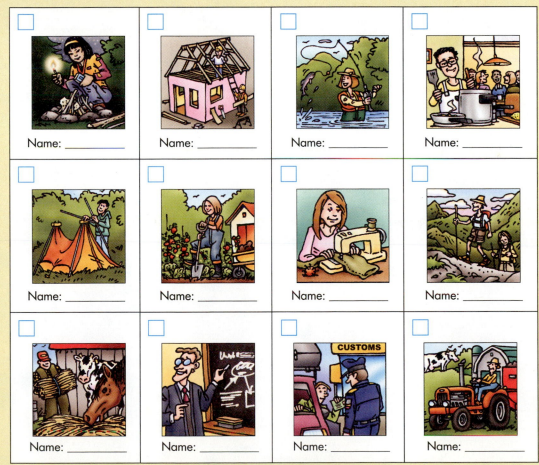

13 Take turns asking *Yes/No* questions to find out what experience your classmates have. When you find someone who answers yes, write the student's name in the appropriate box. The person with the most names filled in at the end of the game is the winner.

World of Music 2

Wonderful Tonight
Eric Clapton

Vocabulary

1 **PAIRS.** Match each verb with the correct word or phrase.

1. ask __c__
2. brush ____
3. feel ____
4. give ____
5. go ____
6. help ____
7. put on ____
8. say ____
9. turn off ____
10. walk around ____

a. "yes"
b. her a present
c. him a question
d. me sit down
e. the lights
f. to a party
g. with me
h. wonderful
i. your hair
j. your makeup

The 70s

*The "British invasion" of rock 'n' roll was in full swing in the 70s. **Eric Clapton**, a guitar virtuoso, became—and remains—one of rock music's most admired stars.*

Listening

2 🎧 Listen to the song. Put the pictures in order.

1. _____ 2. _____ 3. _____

A

B

C

3 🎧 **Listen to the song again. Complete the lyrics.**

Wonderful Tonight

It's late in the evening;
she's wondering what clothes to wear.
She _____ her makeup
and _____ her long blonde hair.
And then she _____ me, "Do I look all right?"
And I _____, "Yes, you look wonderful tonight."

We _____ to a party,
and everyone _____ to see
this beautiful lady
that's _____ around with me.
And then she _____ me, "Do you feel all right?"
and I say, "Yes, I _____ wonderful tonight."

I feel wonderful because I see the love light in your eyes.
And the wonder of it all is that you just don't realize how much I love you.

It's time to _____ home now,
and I've got an aching head.
So I _____ her the car keys,
and she _____ me to bed.

And then I _____ her,
as I _____ the light,
I say, "My darling, you were wonderful tonight.
Oh, my darling, you were wonderful tonight."

4 *PAIRS.* **Compare your answers in Exercise 3.**

Speaking

5 *GROUPS OF 3.* **Discuss the questions.**

What is the song about? Tell the story.
What do you like about the song (for example, the words, the music, the singer's voice)?
Is there something you don't like?

Keepsakes

Vocabulary Possessions; phrasal verbs related to possessions
Grammar Review: possessive *'s*; possessive adjectives/pronouns; *belong to*
Speaking Talking about special possessions

Getting started

1 **Look at the photos of the keepsakes. What do you think *keepsakes* are?**

2 **Match the words in the box with the photos.**

1. ballet shoes __I__   2. baseball glove ___   3. camera ___   4. doll ___

5. jewelry box ___   6. photo album ___   7. pin ___   8. shawl ___

9. toy truck ___   10. watch ___

3 🎧 **Listen and check your answers. Then listen and repeat.**

4 *PAIRS.* **Discuss. What things do you keep as keepsakes?**

Listening

5 **Match the phrasal verbs with their meanings.**

1. give away _g_
2. put away ____
3. try on ____
4. pass on ____
5. take out ____
6. fall apart ____
7. throw away ____
8. fall out ____

a. separate into small pieces
b. wear a piece of clothing for a short time to see if it fits
c. put something in the garbage
d. drop out of the place where it belongs
e. put something in the place where it is usually kept
f. remove something from a place
g. give something to someone instead of selling it
h. give something to someone else

6 🎧 **Mr. Freeman and his young daughter, Lisa, are talking. Listen to their conversation. Circle the letter of the correct answer.**

1. What are Mr. Freeman and Lisa doing?
   a. taking things out of a trunk   b. putting things away in a trunk
2. Are the things old or new?
   a. old   b. new

7 🎧 **Listen again. Match each keepsake in the trunk with the person it belongs (or belonged) to.**

1. jewelry box
2. watch
3. photo album
4. baseball glove

a. Lisa's mother
b. Lisa's father
c. Lisa's grandmother
d. Lisa's grandfather

Pronunciation

8 🎧 **Listen. Notice the stress and linking in these phrasal verbs.**

Take it **out**.   Don't give it a**way**.

It's falling a**part**.   I'll try it **on**.

Let's throw it a**way**.   Wait! Something is falling **out**.

9 🎧 **Listen again and repeat.**

10 *PAIRS.* **Discuss the questions.**

When you don't need something anymore (clothing, books, furniture), what do you do? Do you put it away and keep it, throw it away, or give it away to someone? Why?

Grammar focus

1 Study the examples. Notice the ways to express possession. Notice the use of the apostrophe (').

Possessive *'s*	Possessive adjective	Possessive pronoun	*belong to* + object pronoun
	It's **my** baseball glove.	It's **mine**.	It **belongs to me**.
These are **Grandma's** dolls.	They're **her** dolls.	They're **hers**.	They **belong to her**.
This is **George's** watch.	It's **his** watch.	It's **his**.	It **belongs to him**.
That's the **neighbors'** car.	It's **their** car.	It's **theirs**.	It **belongs to them**.

2 Look at the examples again. Circle the correct words to complete the rules in the chart.

Possessive *'s*; possessive adjectives/pronouns; *belong to*
To show possession:
Use a possessive adjective (*my, your, his, her, our, their*) **before / after** a noun.
Use a possessive pronoun (*mine, yours, his, hers, ours, theirs*) **alone / before a noun**.
Add *'s* to a **singular / plural** noun.
Add *'* to a **singular / plural** noun that ends in *s*.
Use **an object pronoun / a possessive pronoun** after *belong to*.

> **Grammar Reference page 146**

3 Circle the correct words to complete the sentences.

1. That's not her doll. It's **our / (ours)**.
2. This isn't **me / my** sweater. Is it **your / yours**?
3. These are my **parent's / parents'** books.
4. This photo album belongs to **her / she**.
5. My sisters don't like to clean **their / her** room.
6. Is this **her / hers** book? Or is it **him / his**?
7. These old clothes **belong / belongs** to **they / them**.

4 Rewrite the sentences using the words in parentheses.

1. This doll belonged to your grandmother. (your grandmother)
   This was your grandmother's doll.

2. That's my photo album. (belong to)
3. This is your mother's dress. (hers)
4. Their car is very old. (my grandparents)
5. Where is Jason's house? (his)
6. These are our CDs. (belong to)
7. I like to look at her pictures. (Lucia)

Speaking

5 **BEFORE YOU SPEAK.** Imagine you are filling a trunk with keepsakes of the people in your class. Your teacher will give you the name of a classmate. Choose one thing that reminds you of that person, such as a piece of clothing that the person wears a lot or something that the person always has.

6 **GROUPS OF 4.** Talk about the keepsakes that you chose. As a group, agree on one thing to put in the trunk to remember each person by.

A: I think we should put Julia's blue sweater in the trunk. She wears it a lot.
B: No, I think we should put in her cell phone. She loves to talk on the phone after class.

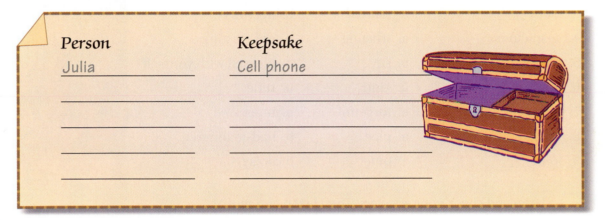

Person	Keepsake
Julia	Cell phone

7 Each group writes the list of keepsakes (with no names!) on the board or reads it to the class. Others in the class guess the people who go with each keepsake. Give reasons.

Anna: The first thing on our list is a cell phone.
José: I think it's yours. You like talking on the phone.
Anna: No, it's not mine.
María: I think it's Julia's. She uses her phone more than anyone!
Anna: You're right. The cell phone belongs to Julia.

Writing

8 Think of a keepsake that belongs to you or to a member of your family. Write a paragraph describing the keepsake and the person, thing, or event it reminds you of. Use possessive forms.

CONVERSATION TO GO

A: Is this **your** phone?
B: No, it's **Susan's**. **Mine** is at home.

UNIT 14

Tales of Nasreddin Hodja

Vocabulary Adjectives describing feelings and behavior
Grammar Adverbs of manner; comparative adverbs
Speaking Describing actions

Lesson A

Getting started

1 Choose the correct synonym for each adjective.

1. upset _a_   a. unhappy   b. happy

2. embarrassed ____   a. comfortable   b. ashamed

3. calm ____   a. relaxed   b. nervous

4. suspicious ____   a. trusting   b. not trusting

5. proud ____   a. shy   b. pleased with yourself

6. polite ____   a. kind   b. rude

7. absent-minded ____   a. forgetful   b. interested

8. rude ____   a. nice   b. bad-mannered

9. loud ____   a. quiet   b. noisy

2 🎧 **Listen and check your answers. Then listen and repeat.**

3 *PAIRS.* **Nasreddin Hodja is a character from Turkish folktales. Look at the pictures. Use adjectives from Exercise 1 to describe how Hodja and the other men look.**

In Picture A, Hodja looks calm, and the men look suspicious.

Reading

4 Think about folktales you know. What's their purpose?

5 Read the stories. Then match the paragraphs with the pictures.

Hodja, the King

One day, Nasreddin Hodja was walking down the road. He was looking at the sky absent-mindedly and not watching where he was going. Suddenly, he bumped into a man. _B_

"Do you know who I am?" the man shouted angrily. "I am the King's advisor!"

"That's very nice," said Hodja calmly. "As for me, I am a king." ____

"A king?" asked the man suspiciously. "What country do you rule?"

"I rule over myself," said Hodja proudly. "I am king of my emotions. I never get angry as you did just now."

The man apologized and walked away quickly, feeling very embarrassed.

Eat, My Coat, Eat

A friend invited Nasreddin Hodja to a banquet. He went to the banquet wearing his everyday clothes. ____

Everyone, including his friend, was very rude to him, so Hodja left quickly. He went back home, put on his best coat, and returned to the banquet. Now everyone greeted him more politely than before and invited him to sit down and eat.

When the soup was served, Hodja put the sleeve of his coat in the bowl. He said loudly, "Eat, my coat, eat!" ____

His friend angrily asked Hodja to stop.

"When I came here in my other clothes," said Hodja calmly, "you treated me badly. But when I returned wearing this fine coat, you gave me the best of everything. So I thought that you wanted my coat, not me, to eat at your banquet!"

6 What lessons do these stories teach? Choose the best answer for each story.

1. "Hodja, the King"
   a. Some people are more important than others.
   b. It is important to control your anger.
   c. Everyone gets angry at times.

2. "Eat, My Coat, Eat"
   a. True friends are not rude to each other.
   b. Wear clothes that are right for the occasion.
   c. Look at the person, not at his or her clothes.

Grammar focus

1 **Study the examples of adverbs of manner.**

> Hodja walked **absent-mindedly** down the road.
> The man walked away **quickly**.
> Everyone greeted him **more politely than** before.
> The man shouted **angrily**.

2 **Look at the examples again. Circle the correct words to complete the chart.**

Adverbs of manner
Use adverbs of manner to describe **how / why** something is done.
Use *more* + adverb + *than* to compare two **actions / things**.
Many adverbs are formed by adding *-ly* to **a verb / an adjective**.
For adjectives ending in *-y,* change the *y* to **a / i** before adding *-ly*.
NOTE: Some adverbs such as *fast, hard,* and *early,* have the same form as adjectives.

> **Grammar Reference page 146**

3 **Complete the sentences with adverbs of manner. Form the adverbs from the adjectives in parentheses.**

1. Nathan walked ___happily___ down the street. (happy)

2. The man sat _____ in front of the house. (quiet)

3. "Where did you go?" the little girl asked the little boy _____. (suspicious)

4. "I designed that building," the architect said _____. (proud)

5. The man shouted _____ at his neighbor. (angry)

4 **Complete the sentences. Use the comparative form of the adverbs in the box. Include *than* when necessary.**

calmly   comfortably   ~~loudly~~   politely   quickly

1. John is quiet. Janet is loud. Janet speaks _more loudly than_ John.

2. Eduardo never rushes. Roberto is always in a hurry. Roberto does everything _____ Eduardo.

3. The salesperson wasn't rude, but the customer was. The salesperson behaved _____ the customer.

4. Sam was angry when he heard the news. Jennifer wasn't upset about the news. Jennifer reacted _____ Sam.

5. Just after his operation my friend was in a lot of pain, but now he's resting _____.

Pronunciation

5 🎧 Listen. Notice the stressed (strong) syllable in each word.

angrily   suspiciously   quietly   comfortably

6 🎧 Listen again. This time, notice the pronunciation of the vowels shown in blue. They all have the short, unclear sound /ə/. Then listen again and repeat.

7 🎧 Now listen to these words. Draw a circle over the stressed syllables and underline the vowels that have the short, unclear sound /ə/.

happily   politely   nervously   hungrily

8 🎧 Listen again and repeat. Check your answers.

Speaking

9 **GROUPS OF 4.** Work together to tell a folktale that teaches something. Decide which folktale you'd like to tell, and take notes. Take turns telling different parts. Add or change parts of the folktale to make it as funny or dramatic as you like.

Folktale:
Characters:
Setting:
Main events:
Ending:
Lesson:

10 Share your folktale with the class. What does each folktale teach?

Writing

11 Write a short story or folktale you know. Use adverbs of manner.

CONVERSATION TO GO

A: You speak **quickly**!
B: No, I don't. You just listen **more slowly** than I speak!

Unit 13 Keepsakes

1 🎧 Listen to the model conversation.

2 Think of a keepsake that you or your family has. Where is it from? What does it look like? Why is it important to you?

3 *PAIRS.* Student A, talk for two minutes. Tell Student B about your keepsake. Explain as many details as you can. Student B, don't ask questions, just listen. Then switch. Student B, talk for two minutes about your keepsake.

4 Change partners. This time you each have only one minute. Talk about the keepsake.

5 Change partners again. This time you each have only thirty seconds. Talk about the keepsake.

Unit 14 Tales of Nasreddin Hodja

6 🎧 Listen to the model conversation.

7 Write each adverb below on a small piece of paper. Fold all the pieces of paper in half, put them in a box, and mix them up.

happily	quickly	calmly	proudly
sadly	angrily	nervously	shyly
slowly	thoughtfully	respectfully	rudely
politely	absent-mindedly	suspiciously	hungrily

8 *GROUPS OF 4.* Make up a group story. Take turns picking a piece of paper. Add two sentences to the story using the adverb on your paper. Continue until all the papers are gone. The person who uses the last adverb finishes the story.

9 Share your stories with the class. Which group has the most unique story?

Unit 2, Exercise 6
Student A

Make these phone calls to Student B. Apologize and make an excuse.

I'm afraid I can't come to work. I have a terrible headache.

1. You have a headache, and you can't go to work. Call your boss.
2. You want to watch a baseball game tonight, but your friend wants you to go to a movie with him/her. Call your friend, Student B, and make an excuse for not going to the movies.
3. Your boss wants you to go out for dinner with a client, but you have a dentist appointment at 6:00. Call your boss, Student B.

Answer these phone calls from Student B. Listen to his/her problems. Show sympathy.

That's too bad.

4. You're an English teacher. Student B is your student.
5. You're a manager in an office. Student B is an employee in your department.
6. You're going to move into your new apartment tomorrow. Student B is your friend.

Review 1, Exercise 10
Student A

Dario is going on a trip. Take turns asking questions to fill in his schedule.

Where is he going to go on Saturday? What's he going to do on Sunday?

Dario's Travel Schedule		8 days/7 nights
Day	**Where**	**What**
Sat.	fly into the city	visit a museum
Sun.	drive down the coast	
Mon.		
Tues.		attend a festival
Wed.	drive to the mountains	
Thurs.		
Fri.		buy souvenirs at a market
Sat.		✕

Unit 6, Exercise 8

Read the email messages and write replies to each one.

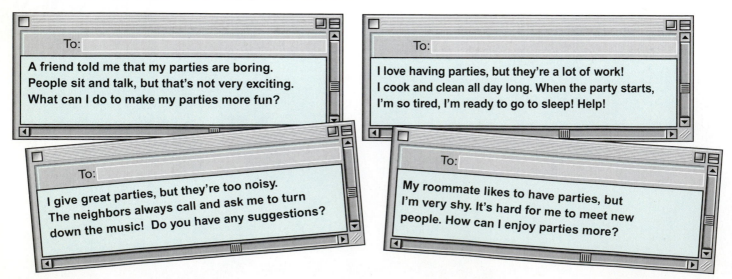

To:

A friend told me that my parties are boring. People sit and talk, but that's not very exciting. What can I do to make my parties more fun?

To:

I love having parties, but they're a lot of work! I cook and clean all day long. When the party starts, I'm so tired, I'm ready to go to sleep! Help!

To:

I give great parties, but they're too noisy. The neighbors always call and ask me to turn down the music! Do you have any suggestions?

To:

My roommate likes to have parties, but I'm very shy. It's hard for me to meet new people. How can I enjoy parties more?

Unit 7, Exercise 6
Student A

Student A, begin. Look at these pictures of your colleagues from another office. Give each person a name. Then describe each one to your partner. Your partner will show you the person in the picture on page 33. Is your partner correct?

A: My colleague, Sandra Vazquez, is going to arrive on Saturday. Can you meet her at the airport?
B: Sure. What does she look like?
A: She . . .

Now, switch roles. Look at page 33.

Review 2, Exercise 8
Student A

Student A, begin. Describe the person in your picture A. Then Student B will describe the person in his or her picture A. Is it the same person? Then Student B continues with picture B.

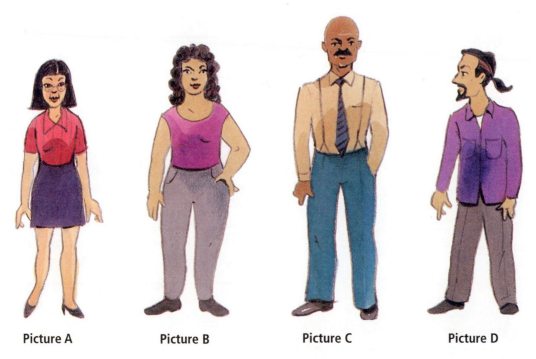

Picture A   Picture B   Picture C   Picture D

Unit 2, Exercise 6
Student B

Answer these phone calls from Student A. Listen to his/her problems. Show sympathy.

That's too bad.

1. You're a supervisor. Student A is your employee.
2. You want to go to the movies tonight. Student A is your friend.
3. You're a supervisor. Student A is your employee.

Make these phone calls to Student A. Apologize and make an excuse.

I'm sorry, but I can't come to class today. I have a fever.

4. You can't go to your English class because you have a fever. Call your teacher, Student A.
5. You have a sore throat and cough. There's an important meeting at work. Call your boss, Student A, and apologize for not going to the meeting.
6. Your friend, Student A, wants you to help him move into a new apartment, but you don't want to. Call your friend and make an excuse.

Review 1, Exercise 10
Student B

Dario is going on a trip. Take turns asking questions to fill in his schedule.

What's he going to do Saturday? Where is he going to go on Sunday?

Dario's Travel Schedule		8 days/7 nights
Day	**Where**	**What**
Sat.	fly into the city	visit a museum
Sun.		go swimming
Mon.	go on safari	
Tues.		
Wed.		go hiking
Thurs.	take a bus to the lake	
Fri.		buy souvenirs at a market
Sat.	fly home	

Review 7, Exercise 2
Student A

Look at the chart. Ask questions to find out how well each athlete could do sports ten years ago. (Don't look at your partner's chart.)

Athlete	Sport	10 years ago
Lise	🏊	–
	🤽	– –
	🏃	+
Ho-Jin	🤼	
	🏋	
	🏃	
Flavia	🏃	+ +
	🏊	+
	🥊	– –
Simon	🏃	
	🏃	
	🏋	

Symbol	Meaning	
+++	could . . . really well	be really good at . . .
++	could . . . well	be good at . . .
+	could . . . pretty well	be pretty good at . . .
–	couldn't . . . very well	be not very good at . . .
– –	couldn't . . . at all	be no good at . . .

Student B, look at these pictures of your colleagues from another office. Give each person a name. Then describe each one to your partner. Your partner will show you the person in the picture on page 33. Is your partner correct?

B: *My colleague, Carlos Lopez, is going to arrive on Saturday. Can you meet him at the airport?*
A: *Sure. What does he look like?*
B: *He…*

Review 2, Exercise 8
Student B

Student A will describe the person in his or her picture A. Then you will describe the person in your picture A. Is it the same person? Then continue with picture B.

Picture A   Picture B   Picture C   Picture D

Unit 6, Exercise 6

Look at the costs in the worksheet. Put a check (✓) next to your suggestions.

Party Planning Worksheet

		Cost	Check (✓)
Location	At school/home/the office	$0	
	Hotel	$150	
Food and beverages	Snacks (chips, cheese, sandwiches, soft drinks)	$75	
	Buffet dinner with soft drinks	$150	
	Formal dinner with soft drinks and wine	$275	
	Dessert buffet	$100	
	Ice cream	$50	
	Cookies	$30	
Music	Band	$150	
	DJ	$75	
	CD player	$0	
Entertainment	Photographer	$75	
	Games	$100	
	Celebrity guest	$300	
	Total:		

Review 4, Exercise 13
Student A

Student A, you're at the supermarket. Call Student B to ask what you should buy.

Switch roles. Student A, look at the food in the picture. Tell Student B what food you have at home and suggest what he or she needs to buy.

Unit 18, Exercise 7

There were 16 people in the picture on page 85. Try to answer these questions about each person:

• What were they doing?
• What were they wearing?
• Where were they in the picture?

A man was chasing his dog. He was wearing a red jacket.

Unit 22, Exercise 7
Student A

Use the phrases to make your requests and offers.

Requests	Offers
Can you…?	Would you like me to…?
Could you…?	Should I…?
	I'll…

A: Can you do the filing, please?
B: Yes, of course. I'll do it this afternoon.

• **Situation 1**
  You're an executive at a television station. Student B is your assistant. Ask Student B to:
  a. send a fax.
  b. make a dinner reservation at the Lemon Tree Restaurant.
  c. type a letter.

• **Situation 2**
  You're a shoe salesperson in a department store. Student B is the store manager.
  a. You're waiting on a customer. Your boss asks you to do something. Offer to do the task after you finish with the customer.
  b. You hurt your back on the weekend. You think Bob (another salesperson) can help. Offer to ask Bob.
  c. You're going to the sandwich shop for lunch. Your boss asks you to do something. Offer to do the task after lunch.

Review 7, Exercise 2
Student B

Look at the chart. Ask questions to find out how well each athlete could do sports ten years ago. (Don't look at your partner's chart.)

Athlete	Sport	10 years ago
Lise		
Ho-Jin		+ +
		+
		–
Flavia		
Simon		+ +
		+
		–

Symbol	Meaning	
+++	could . . . really well	be really good at . . .
++	could . . . well	be good at . . .
+	could . . . pretty well	be pretty good at . . .
–	couldn't . . . very well	be not very good at . . .
– –	couldn't . . . at all	be no good at . . .

Unit 22, Exercise 7
Student B

Use the phrases to make your requests and offers.

Requests	Offers
Can you . . . ?	Would you like me to . . . ?
Could you . . . ?	Should I . . . ?
	I'll . . .

A: *Can you do the filing, please?*
B: *Yes, of course. I'll do it this afternoon.*

- **Situation 1**
  You're an administrative assistant at a television station. Student A is your boss. Use this information when your boss makes a request:
  a. The fax machine is broken. Offer to send an email instead.
  b. The Lemon Tree Restaurant is closed. Offer to try some other restaurants.
  c. You're busy typing a report. Your boss asks you to do something. Offer to do the task after you finish the report.

- **Situation 2**
  You're the manager of a department store. Student A is a salesperson in the shoe department. Ask Student A to:
  a. put the shoes back in the storeroom.
  b. help you move a large box.
  c. put *Sale* signs on certain shoe racks.

Unit 9, Exercise 7
Students B and C

You are customers at Rosie's Restaurant. Look at the menu. Decide what you would like and give your order to your waiter/waitress.

Waiter: Would you like to order?
Customer: Yes. I'd like the chicken in herb sauce.

Rosie's Restaurant

Appetizers	Cup	Bowl
Tomato soup	$3.25	$4.00
Chicken soup	$3.25	$4.00
Soup of the day	$3.25	$4.00

Entrées	
Pasta with tomato sauce	$8.95
Pasta with garlic sauce	$9.95
Chicken in herb sauce	$12.95
Shrimp with vegetables	$15.95

Side dishes	
French fries	$2.25
Garden salad	$2.95
Mixed vegetables	$2.75
Rice	$2.25

Desserts	
Ice cream	$3.00
Chocolate or vanilla	
Cake	$4.25
Cheesecake	$5.00

Review 4, Exercise 13
Student B

Student B, look at the food in the picture. Tell Student A what food you have at home and suggest what he or she needs to buy.

Switch roles. Student B, you're at the supermarket. Call Student A to ask what you should buy. Write a shopping list.

Review 1, Exercise 10
Student C

Dario is going on a trip. take turns asking questions to fill in his schedule.

Where is he going to go on Sunday? What is he going to do on Saturday?

Dario's Travel Schedule		8 days/7 nights
Day	**Where**	**What**
Sat.	fly into the city	
Sun.		
Mon.		see elephants and lions
Tues.	visit the countryside	
Wed.		
Thurs.		do water sports
Fri.	return to the city	
Sat.		✕

Grammar reference

Unit 1

Simple present and adverbs of frequency

- Use **how often** to ask about frequency.
  How often do you go to the movies?
  How often does Mary visit you?

- Use adverbs of frequency (**never, sometimes, usually, often, always**) with the present tense to say how often something happens.
  Do they **always** go out on Saturday?
  She **usually** goes to a café.
  Peter doesn't **often** watch TV.
  We **sometimes** get takeout.
  I **never** work late.

Notes:

- Adverbs of frequency go after the verb **be**, but before all other verbs.
  It**'s always** noisy.
  John **often runs** after work.

- The adverb **sometimes** can also go at the beginning of a sentence.
  Sometimes we get takeout.

Unit 2

Linking words: *and, but, so*

- Use the words **and**, **but**, and **so** to connect ideas.
- Use **and** to connect similar ideas.
  I have a headache, **and** my stomach hurts. (I have two problems.)
- Use **but** to connect different ideas.
  I have a headache, **but** my stomach feels okay. (I only have one problem: a headache.)
- Use **so** to show a result.
  I took some aspirin, **so** I feel better. (I feel better because I took aspirin.)

Unit 3

Simple past: regular and irregular verbs

- Use the simple past to talk about completed actions in the past, often with a specific time reference (*in 1990, yesterday, last year*, etc.).

- Add **–d** or **–ed** to regular verbs to form the simple past in affirmative statements.
  A television station **hired** her.
  She **wanted** to be famous.

- Some verbs are irregular in the simple past. (See the list on page 150.)
  She **got** a job in television.
  People **began** to notice her.

Negative	Subject + **didn't** + base form of the verb She **didn't finish** college. Her parents **didn't have** a lot of money.
Question	**Did** + subject + base form of the verb **Did** people **like** her television program? **Did** she **make** movies?
Short answers	**Yes** + subject + **did** **Yes**, she **did**.
	No + subject + **didn't** **No**, she **didn't**.

Unit 4

Be going to for future

- Use **be going to** to talk about future plans.

Affirmative	Subject + **be going to** + base form of the verb I**'m going to see** the Rocky Mountains. It**'s going to be** crowded there.
Negative	Subject + **be** + **not** + **going to** + base form of the verb You**'re not going to travel** with me. I**'m not going to take** a lot of stuff.
Question	**Be** + subject + **going to** + base form of the verb **Is** the weather **going to be** sunny? **Are** the markets **going to be** open?
Short answers	**Yes** + subject + **be** **Yes**, it **is**.
	No + subject + **be** + **not** **No**, it **isn't**.

Notes:

- The form of **be** must agree with the subject.
  I am going to travel.
  You aren't going to snorkel.
  She's going to speak English.
  We're going to go on a safari.
  They're going to sightsee.

- You can use the present continuous **going to** instead of **going to go** to talk about traveling.
  We're going to go to India.
  We're going to India.

Unit 5

Modals: *should* and *shouldn't* for advice
• Use ***should*** to give and ask for advice.

Affirmative	Subject + **should** + base form of the verb *You **should** shake hands.* *She **should** take a gift.*
Negative	Subject + **shouldn't** + base form of the verb *We **shouldn't** take our shoes off.* *They **shouldn't** arrive late.*
Question	**Should** + subject + base form of the verb ***Should** we shake hands?* ***Should** she use first names?*
Short answers	**Yes** + subject + **should** **Yes**, *you* **should**.
	No + subject + **shouldn't** **No**, *she* **shouldn't**.

Unit 6

Expressions for making suggestions

Use ***why don't, let's (not), maybe ... could,*** and ***how about*** to make suggestions.

• ***Why don't*** + subject + base form of the verb
  *Why **don't** we have a party?*
  *Why **don't** you come?*
• ***Let's (not)*** + base form of the verb
  ***Let's** take something.*
  ***Let's not** make salad.*
• ***Maybe*** + subject + ***could***
  ***Maybe** you **could** take drinks.*
  ***Maybe** he **could** get ice.*
• ***How about*** + verb + *–ing*
  ***How about** playing some games?*
  ***How about** listening to some music?*

Unit 7

Be and *have* with physical descriptions

• Use ***be*** to talk about people's ages.
  *I'm 34. How old **are** you?*
• Use ***be*** to talk about people's height.
  *You **are** short, and he **is** average height.*
• Use ***be*** to talk about people's weight.
  *She **is** slim, but her sisters **are** heavy.*

• Use ***have*** to talk about people's eyes.
  *Ben and Jeff **have** green eyes, but Ann **has** blue eyes.*
• Use ***have*** to talk about people's hair.
  *She **has** long hair, but he **has** short hair.*
• Use ***have*** to talk about people's facial hair.
  *Keith **has** a moustache, but he **doesn't have** a beard.*

Exception: Use ***be*** with ***bald***.
*Ken has thick hair, but his father **is** bald.*

Unit 8

Say and *tell*

• ***Say*** and ***tell*** are irregular verbs in the simple past.
  *say → **said**   tell → **told***
• Always use an object pronoun (***me, you, him, her, it, us, them***) or a noun with ***told***.
  *I **told you** that I saw the movie.*
  *You **told me** that you didn't like it.*
  *He told **John** about making movies.*
• Never use an object pronoun or noun with ***said***.
  *She **said** that she loved Dr. No.*
  *We **said** that Halle Berry was a great actress.*
• Use the present after ***say*** or ***tell*** and the past after ***said*** or ***told***.
  *She **says** that Casablanca **is** a good movie.*
  *She **said** that she **liked** black-and-white films.*
  *He **tells** me that Star Wars **is** his favorite movie.*
  *He **told** me that he **loved** the special effects.*

Note: You don't have to use the word ***that*** with ***say*** or ***tell***.
She said she liked black-and-white films.
He told me he loved the special effects.

Unit 9

Would like/like, would prefer/prefer

- Use *like* and *prefer* to talk about the things you usually like.
  I *like* shrimp.
  He *likes* going out to dinner.
  We *prefer* red wine to white.
  She *prefers* small restaurants to large ones.
- Use *would like* and *would prefer* to talk about the things that you want at this moment or in the future.
  Would you like a drink?
  I'd like a glass of water, please.
  Would you prefer the chicken or the shrimp?
  We'*d prefer* the chicken tonight, thanks.

Notes:
- Use the contraction '*d* for *would* in affirmative sentences.
  I'*d like* the fish.
  We'*d prefer* red wine.
- Use *prefer* to show a choice between two things.
  Prefer is usually used in negative sentences.
  I *prefer* juice to soda.

Unit 10

Will for predicting

- Use *will* and *will not (won't)* to make predictions about the future.

Affirmative	Subject + *will* ('*ll*) + base form of the verb People *will* travel more. We'*ll* take vacations to the moon.
Negative	Subject + *will not (won't)* + base form of the verb People *won't* use cars as much. We *won't* pollute the environment.
Question	*Will* + subject + base form of the verb *Will* types of transportation change? *Will* the population of the world increase?
Short answers	*Yes* + subject + *will* *Yes*, it *will*.
	No + subject + *won't* *No*, it *won't*.

- Also use *I think* and *I don't think* with *will/won't* to make predictions about the future.
  I think we'*ll* use the Internet more.
  I think people *won't* write letters anymore.
  I don't think there *will* be hotels in space.
  Do you think we'*ll* fly private jets instead of driving cars?

Note: When using *I think* with *will/won't*, be careful to form negatives and short answers correctly. (*Think* is in the present.)

I don't think *I'll* go.
X I think I won't go.

Do you think *we'll* survive?
Yes, I do.
X Yes, I will.

Unit 11

Have to/don't have to

- Use *have to* to say that something is necessary.
  I *have to* get up early to go to work. (It's necessary.)
  I *don't have to* get up early on Sundays. (It's not necessary.)
  Do you *have to* use a computer at work?

Affirmative	Subject + *have/has to* + base form of the verb I *have to* work a lot. She *has to* travel for her job.
Negative	Subject + *don't/doesn't have to* + base form of the verb Doctors *don't have to* sell things. The salesperson *doesn't have to* type.
Question	*Do/Does* + subject *have to* + base form of the verb *Do* you *have to* work on weekends? *Does* your boss *have to* review your work?
Short answers	*Yes* + subject + *do/does* *Yes*, she *does*.
	No + subject + *don't/doesn't* *No*, she *doesn't*.

Note: Use *do/does* (not *have/has*) in short answers.

Do you have to work late?
Yes, I *do*.
X Yes, I have.
No, I *don't*.
X No, I haven't.

Grammar reference

Unit 12

Present perfect for indefinite past: *ever, never*

- Use the present perfect to talk about events that happened at an unspecified time in the past.

Affirmative	Subject + **have/has** + past participle I **have traveled** a lot. He **has spent** time outdoors.
Negative	Subject + **haven't/hasn't** + past participle We **haven't worked** on a farm. She **hasn't grown** food.
Question	**Have/has** + subject + past participle **Have** you **lived** overseas? **Has** it **rained** a lot?
Short answers	**Yes** + subject + **have/has** **Yes**, I **have**. **Yes**, it **has**.
	No + subject + **haven't/hasn't** **No**, I **haven't**. **No**, it **hasn't**.

- Use *ever* to make a question with the present perfect.
  *Have you **ever** traveled overseas?*
- Use *not* or *never* to make a negative statement with the present perfect.
  *No, I have**n't**. I have **never** traveled overseas.*

Note: To form the past participle of regular verbs, add *–d* or *–ed* to the base form of the verb. There is a list of irregular verbs on page 150.

Unit 13

Review: possessive *'s*

- Use *'s* after people's names or singular nouns to show possession.
  *They're the family**'s** photos.*
  *It's not Lisa**'s** jewelry box.*
  *Where is James**'s** watch?*
- Use *'* after regular plural nouns to show possession.
  *That is my grandparents**'** trunk.*
  *The boys**'** photos are in the album.*
- Use *'s* after irregular plural nouns.
  *The children**'s** toys are upstairs.*
  *Where are the women**'s** dresses?*

Possessive adjectives

- Use possessive adjectives (*my, your, his, her, its, our, their*) to replace a possessive noun in a sentence.
  *This is Paul's guitar. → This is **his** guitar.*
  *That is the dog's bed. → That is **its** bed.*

Note: it's = it is; its = possessive adjective

Possessive pronouns

- Use possessive pronouns (*mine, yours, his, hers, ours, theirs*) to replace a possessive adjective and the noun it describes.
  *They're my books. → They're **mine**.*
  *It's our house. → It's **ours**.*

Belong to

- Use the verb ***belong to*** to talk about things that a person has or owns.
  *The book **belongs to** me. (I own the book.)*
  *The dolls **belong to** Cindy. (Cindy owns the dolls.)*

Unit 14

Adverbs of manner; comparative adverbs

- Use adverbs of manner to tell how an action is done.
  *You asked **rudely**, but I answered **politely**.*
- Many adverbs of manner are formed by adding *–ly* to an adjective.
  *proud → proud**ly***
  *polite → polite**ly***
  *kind → kind**ly***
  *suspicious → suspicious**ly***
- Use ***more/less*** + adverb of manner + ***than*** to compare two actions.
  *Mapela talks **more quickly than** Haneko.*
  *Haneko talks **more slowly than** Mapela.*

Notes:

- For adjectives ending in *–y*, change the **y** to *i*, then add *–ly*.
  happy → happ**ily**
  angry → angr**ily**
- **Well** is the adverb form of **good**.
  *Mahala is a **good** singer.*
  *Mahala sings **well**.*

Irregular Verbs

Simple present	Simple past	Past participle	Simple present	Simple past	Past participle
be	was/were	been	ride	rode	ridden
become	became	become	read	read	read
begin	began	begun	run	ran	run
break	broke	broken	say	said	said
build	built	built	see	saw	seen
buy	bought	bought	sell	sold	sold
catch	caught	caught	send	sent	sent
choose	chose	chose	shake	shook	shaken
come	came	come	show	showed	shown
cost	cost	cost	sing	sang	sung
do	did	done	sit	sat	sat
draw	drew	drawn	sleep	slept	slept
drink	drank	drunk	speak	spoke	spoken
drive	drove	driven	spend	spent	spent
eat	ate	eaten	stand	stood	stood
fall	fell	fallen	swim	swam	swum
feel	felt	felt	take	took	taken
fight	fought	fought	teach	taught	taught
find	found	found	tell	told	told
fly	flew	flown	think	thought	thought
forget	forgot	forgotten	throw	threw	thrown
get	got	gotten	understand	understood	understood
give	gave	given	wear	wore	worn
go	went	gone	win	won	won
grow	grew	grown	write	wrote	written
hang	hung	hung			
have	had	had			
hear	heard	heard			
hurt	hurt	hurt			
keep	kept	kept			
know	knew	known			
leave	left	left			
lend	lent	lent			
lose	lost	lost			
make	made	made			
mean	meant	meant			
meet	met	met			
pay	paid	paid			
put	put	put			
quit	quit	quit			

Vocabulary

Unit 1
get takeout
go for a walk
go out for dinner
go to the beach
go to the gym
go to the movies
meet friends
rent a video
sleep late
stay home
watch TV
work late

Unit 2
arm
back
ear
eye
foot
hand
head
leg
mouth
nose
stomach
throat
a cold
a cough
a fever
a headache
a sore throat
a stomachache
I hurt my . . . .
My . . . is/are sore.

Unit 3
be born
find a job
get married
give money to charity
go to school
graduate from school
grow up
have children
work hard

Unit 4
Australia
Africa
Asia
Canada
England
Europe
India
Ireland
Italy
Korea
North America
South Africa
coast
countryside
market
monuments
mountains
safari

Unit 5
arrive on time
bow
exchange business cards
give a gift
kiss
shake hands
take a flowers
take your shoes off
use first names/last names
visit someone's home
wear a suit

Unit 6
a birthday party
a costume party
a going-away party
afford
buy
cost
pay
rent
spend

Unit 7
age
elderly
middle-aged
young
height
average height
short
tall
weight
average weight
heavy
slim
hair
black
blond
brown
curly
dark
bald
beard
long
mustache/moustache
sideburns
straight

Unit 8
action movie
comedy
science fiction movie
romantic film
actress
actor
director
special effects
scenery
amazing
black-and-white film
classic
excellent
exciting
fantastic
fast
good
interesting
slow

Unit 9

customer
waiter
menu
appetizer
entree
side dish
cappuccino
coffee
espresso
tea
dessert
cheesecake
chocolate ice cream
raspberry sorbet
fork
glass
knife
napkin
pepper
salt
spoon
garden salad
herbs
mixed vegetables
olives
pasta
rice
sauce
shrimp
soup of the day
tomatoes

Unit 10

climate
communication
economy
government
politics
population
prediction
space
technology
transportation

Unit 11

arrange meetings
communicate
give presentations
make decisions
make money
meet with clients
travel
type letters and contracts
wait on customers
work as a team
work long hours

Unit 12

build a house
catch a fish
cook for a group
grow food
have an adventure
make clothes
spend time
start a business
take care of animals
teach a class
travel abroad
use a computer
work on a farm
write an article

Unit 13

ballet shoes
baseball glove
camera
doll
jewelry box
photo album
pin
shawl
toy truck
watch
fall apart
fall out
give away
pass on
put away
throw away
take out
try on

Unit 14

absent-minded
ashamed
bad-mannered
calm
embarrassed
forgetful
loud
polite
proud
relaxed
rude
suspicious
trusting
upset

Acknowledgments

The authors and series editor wish to acknowledge with gratitude the following reviewers, consultants, and piloters for their thoughtful contributions to the development of *WorldView*.

BRAZIL: São Paulo: Sérgio Gabriel, **FMU/Cultura Inglesa, Jundiaí;** Heloísa Helena Medeiros Ramos, **Kiddy and Teen;** Zaina Nunes, Márcia Mathias Pinto, Angelita Goulvea Quevedo, **Pontifícia Universidade Católica;** Rosa Laquimia Souza, **FMU-FIAM;** Élcio Camilo Alves de Souza, Marie Adele Ryan, **Associação Alumni;** Maria Antonieta Gagliardi, **Centro Britânico;** Chris Ritchie, Debora Schisler, Sandra Natalini, **Sevenidiomas;** Joacyr Oliveira, **FMU;** Maria Thereza Garrelhas Gentil, **Colégio Mackenzie;** Carlos Renato Lopes, **Uni-Santana;** Yara M. Bannwart Rago, **Associação Escola Graduada de São Paulo;** Jacqueline Zilberman, **Instituto King's Cross;** Vera Lúcia Cardoso Berk, **Talkative Idioms Center;** Ana Paula Hoepers, **Instituto Winners;** Carlos C.S. de Celis, Daniel Martins Neto, **CEL-LEP;** Maria Carmen Castellani, **União Cultural Brasil Estados Unidos;** Kátia Martins P. de Moraes Leme, **Colégio Pueri Domus;** Luciene Martins Farias, **Aliança Brasil Estados Unidos;** Neide Aparecida Silva, **Cultura Inglesa;** Áurea Shinto, **Santos:** Maria Lúcia Bastos, **Instituto Four Seasons. COLOMBIA: Bogota:** Sergio Monguí, Rafael Díaz Morales, **Universidad de la Salle;** Yecid Ortega Páez, Yojanna Ruiz G., **Universidad Javeriana;** Merry García Metzger, **Universidad Minuto de Dios;** Maria Caterina Barbosa, **Coninglés;** Nelson Martínez R., **Asesorías Académicas;** Eduardo Martínez, Stella Lozano Vega, **Universidad Santo Tomás de Aquino;** Kenneth McIntyre, **ABC English Institute. JAPAN: Tokyo:** Peter Bellars, **Obirin University;** Michael Kenning, **Takushoku University;** Martin Meldrum, **Takushoku University;** Carol Ann Moritz, **New International School;** Mary Sandkamp, **Musashi Sakai;** Dan Thompson, **Yachiyo Chiba-ken/American Language Institute;** Carol Vaughn, **Kanto Kokusai High School. Osaka:** Lance Burrows, **Osaka Prefecture Settsu High School;** Bonnie Carpenter, **Mukogawa Joshi Daigaku/ Hannan Daigaku;** Josh Glaser, Richard Roy, **Human International University/Osaka Jogakuin Junior College;** Gregg Kennerly, **Osaka YMCA;** Ted Ostis, **Otemon University;** Chris Page, **ECC Language Institute;** Leon Pinsky, **Kwansei Gakuin University;** Chris Ruddenklau, **Kinki University;** John Smith, **Osaka International University. Saitama:** Marie Cosgrove, **Surugadai University. Kobe:** Donna Fujimoto, **Kobe University of Commerce. KOREA: Seoul:** Adrienne Edwards-Daugherty, Min Hee Kang, James Kirkmeyer, Paula Reynolds, Warren Weappa, Matthew Williams, **YBM ELS Shinchon;** Brian Cook, Jack Scott, Russell Tandy, **Hanseoung College. MEXICO: Mexico City:** Alberto Hern, **Instituto Anglo Americano de Idiomas;** Eugenia Carbonell, **Universidad Interamericana;** Cecilia Rey Gutiérrez, María del Rosario Escalada Ruiz, **Universidad Motolinia;** Raquel Márquez Colin, **Universidad St. John's;** Francisco Castillo, Carlos René Malacara Ramos, **CELE – UNAM/Mascarones;** Belem Saint Martin, **Preparatoria ISEC;** María Guadalupe Aguirre Hernández, **Comunidad Educativa Montessori;** Isel Vargas Ruelas, Patricia Contreras, **Centro Universitario Oparin;** Gabriela Juárez Hernández, Arturo Vergara Esteban Juan, **English Fast Center;** Jesús Armando Martínez Salgado, **Preparatoria Leon Tolstoi;** Regina Peña Martínez, **Centro Escolar Anahuac;** Guadalupe Buenrostro, **Colegio Partenon;** Rosendo Rivera Sánchez, **Colegio Anglo Español;** María Rosario Hernández Reyes, **Escuela Preparatoria Monte Albán;** Fernanda Cruzado, **Instituto Tecnológico del Sur;** Janet Harris M., **Colegio Anglo Español;** Rosalba Pérez Contreras, **Centro Lingüístico Empresarial. Ecatepec:** Diana Patricia Ordaz García, **Comunidad Educativa Montessori;** Leticia Ricart P., **Colegio Holandés;** Samuel Hernández B. **Instituto Cultural Renacimiento. Tlalpan:** Ana María Cortés, **Centro Educativo José P. Cacho. San Luis Potosi:** Sigi Orta Hernández, María de Guadalupe Barrientos J., **Instituto Hispano Inglés;** Antonieta Raya Z., **Instituto Potosino;** Gloria Carpizo, **Seminario Mayor Arquidiocesano de San Luis Potosí;** Susana Prieto Noyola, Silvia Yolanda Ortiz Romo **Universidad Politécnica de San Luis Potosí;** Rosa Arrendondo Flores, **Instituto Potosino/Universidad Champagnat;** María Cristina Carmillo, María Carmen García Leos, **Departamento Universitario de Inglés, UASLP;** María Gloria Candia Castro, **Universidad Tecnológica SLP;** Bertha Guadalupe Garza Treviño, **Centro de Idiomas, UASLP. Guadalajara:** Nancy Patricia Gómez Ley, **Escuela Técnica Palmares;** Gabriela Michel Vázquez, **Colegio Cervantes Costa Rica;** Abraham Barbosa Martínez, **Colegio Enrique de Osso;** Ana Cristina Plascencia Haro, Joaquín Limón Ramos, **Centro Educativo Tlaquepaque III;** Lucía Huerta Cervantes, Paulina Cervantes Fernández, Audrey Lizaola López, **Colegio Enrique de Osso,** Rocío de Miguel, **Colegio La Paz;** Jim Nixon, **Colegio Cervantes Costa Rica;** Hilda Delgado Parga, **Colegio D'Monaco;** Claudia Rodríguez, **English Key. León:** Laura Montes de la Serna, **Colegio Británico A.C.;** Antoinette Marie Hernández, **"The Place 4U2 Learn" Language School;** Delia Zavala Torres, Verónica Medellín Urbina, **EPCA Sur;** María Eugenia Gutiérrez Mena, Ana Paulina Suárez Cervantes, **Universidad la Salle;** Herlinda Rodríguez Hernández, **Instituto Mundo Verde,** María Rosario Torres Neri, **Instituto Jassa. Aguascalientes:** María Dolores Jiménez Chávez, **ECA – Universidad Autónoma de Aguascalientes;** María Aguirre Hernández, **ECA – Proyecto Start;** Fernando Xavier Goúrey O., **UAA – IEA "Keep On";** Felisia Guadalupe García Ruiz, **Universidad Tecnológica;** Margarita Zapiain B, Martha Ayala de la Concordia, Fernando Xavier Gomez Orenday, **Universidad Autónoma de Aguascalientes;** Gloria Aguirre Hernández, **Escuela de la Ciudad de Aguascalientes;** Hector Arturo Moreno Diaz, **Universidad Bonaterra.**

SINGLE PC LICENSE AGREEMENT AND LIMITED WARRANTY

READ THIS LICENSE CAREFULLY BEFORE OPENING THIS PACKAGE. BY OPENING THIS PACKAGE, YOU ARE AGREEING TO THE TERMS AND CONDITIONS OF THIS LICENSE. IF YOU DO NOT AGREE, DO NOT OPEN THE PACKAGE. PROMPTLY RETURN THE UNOPENED PACKAGE AND ALL ACCOMPANYING ITEMS TO THE PLACE YOU OBTAINED THEM FOR A FULL REFUND OF ANY SUMS YOU HAVE PAID FOR THE SOFTWARE. ***THESE TERMS APPLY TO ALL LICENSED SOFTWARE ON THE DISK.***

1. **GRANT OF LICENSE and OWNERSHIP:** The enclosed computer programs ("Software") are licensed, not sold, to you by Pearson Education, Inc. publishing as Pearson Longman ("We" or the "Company") and in consideration of your payment of the license fee, which is part of the price you paid of your purchase or adoption of the accompanying Company textbooks and/or other materials, and your agreement to these terms. We reserve any rights not granted to you. You own only the disk(s) but we and/or our licensors own the Software itself. This license allows you to use and display your copy of the Software on a single computer (i.e., with a single CPU) at a single location for academic use only, so long as you comply with the terms of this Agreement. You may make one copy for back up, or transfer your copy to another CPU, provided that the Software is usable on only one computer.

2. **RESTRICTIONS:** You may not transfer or distribute the Software or documentation to anyone else. Except for backup, you may not copy the documentation or the Software. Except as you are otherwise expressly permitted in writing by Pearson, you may not network the Software or otherwise use it on more than one computer or computer terminal at the same time. You may not reverse engineer, disassemble, decompile, modify, adapt, translate, or create derivative works based on the Software or the Documentation. You may be held legally responsible for any copying or copyright infringement that is caused by your failure to abide by the terms of these restrictions.

3. **TERMINATION:** This license is effective until terminated. This license will terminate automatically without notice from the Company if you fail to comply with any provisions or limitations of this license. Upon termination, you shall destroy the Documentation and all copies of the Software. All provisions of this Agreement as to limitation and disclaimer of warranties, limitation of liability, remedies or damages, and our ownership rights shall survive termination.

4. **LIMITED WARRANTY AND DISCLAIMER OF WARRANTY:** Company warrants that for a period of 60 days from the date you purchase this SOFTWARE (or purchase or adopt the accompanying textbook), the Software, when properly installed and used in accordance with the Documentation, will operate in substantial conformity with the description of the Software set forth in the Documentation, and that for a period of 30 days the disk(s) on which the Software is delivered shall be free from defects in materials and workmanship under normal use. The Company does not warrant that the Software will meet your requirements or that the operation of the Software will be uninterrupted or error-free. Your only remedy and the Company's only obligation under these limited warranties is, at the Company's option, return of the disk for a refund of any amounts paid for it by you or replacement of the disk. THIS LIMITED WARRANTY IS THE ONLY WARRANTY PROVIDED BY THE COMPANY AND ITS LICENSORS, AND THE COMPANY AND ITS LICENSORS DISCLAIM ALL OTHER WARRANTIES, EXPRESS OR IMPLIED, INCLUDING WITHOUT LIMITATION, THE IMPLIED WARRANTIES OF MERCHANTABILITY AND FITNESS FOR A PARTICULAR PURPOSE. THE COMPANY DOES NOT WARRANT, GUARANTEE OR MAKE ANY REPRESENTATION REGARDING THE ACCURACY, RELIABILITY, CURRENTNESS, USE, OR RESULTS OF USE, OF THE SOFTWARE.

5. **LIMITATION OF REMEDIES AND DAMAGES:** IN NO EVENT, SHALL THE COMPANY OR ITS EMPLOYEES, AGENTS, LICENSORS, OR CONTRACTORS BE LIABLE FOR ANY INCIDENTAL, INDIRECT, SPECIAL, OR CONSEQUENTIAL DAMAGES ARISING OUT OF OR IN CONNECTION WITH THIS LICENSE OR THE SOFTWARE, INCLUDING FOR LOSS OF USE, LOSS OF DATA, LOSS OF INCOME OR PROFIT, OR OTHER LOSSES, SUSTAINED AS A RESULT OF INJURY TO ANY PERSON, OR LOSS OF OR DAMAGE TO PROPERTY, OR CLAIMS OF THIRD PARTIES, EVEN IF THE COMPANY OR AN AUTHORIZED REPRESENTATIVE OF THE COMPANY HAS BEEN ADVISED OF THE POSSIBILITY OF SUCH DAMAGES. IN NO EVENT SHALL THE LIABILITY OF THE COMPANY FOR DAMAGES WITH RESPECT TO THE SOFTWARE EXCEED THE AMOUNTS ACTUALLY PAID BY YOU, IF ANY, FOR THE SOFTWARE OR THE ACCOMPANYING TEXTBOOK. BECAUSE SOME JURISDICTIONS DO NOT ALLOW THE LIMITATION OF LIABILITY IN CERTAIN CIRCUMSTANCES, THE ABOVE LIMITATIONS MAY NOT ALWAYS APPLY TO YOU.

6. **GENERAL:** THIS AGREEMENT SHALL BE CONSTRUED IN ACCORDANCE WITH THE LAWS OF THE UNITED STATES OF AMERICA AND THE STATE OF NEW YORK, APPLICABLE TO CONTRACTS MADE IN NEW YORK, EXCLUDING THE STATE'S LAWS AND POLICIES ON CONFLICTS OF LAW, AND SHALL BENEFIT THE COMPANY, ITS AFFILIATES AND ASSIGNEES. THIS AGREEMENT IS THE COMPLETE AND EXCLUSIVE STATEMENT OF THE AGREEMENT BETWEEN YOU AND THE COMPANY AND SUPERSEDES ALL PROPOSALS OR PRIOR AGREEMENTS, ORAL, OR WRITTEN, AND ANY OTHER COMMUNICATIONS BETWEEN YOU AND THE COMPANY OR ANY REPRESENTATIVE OF THE COMPANY RELATING TO THE SUBJECT MATTER OF THIS AGREEMENT. If you are a U.S. Government user, this Software is licensed with "restricted rights" as set forth in subparagraphs (a)-(d) of the Commercial Computer-Restricted Rights clause at FAR 52.227-19 or in subparagraphs (c)(1)(ii) of the Rights in Technical Data and Computer Software clause at DFARS 252.227-7013, and similar clauses, as applicable.

How to Start the CD-ROM
This CD-ROM does not require an installation. The CD-ROM must be in the CD-ROM drive while using the program.

For Windows:
1. For optimal display, we recommend that your monitor be set with 800 x 600 resolution.

2. Insert the CD-ROM into the computer's CD-ROM drive.

3. The program should begin automatically.

4. If the program does not begin automatically, open "My Computer," and then double-click on the *WorldView* CD-ROM icon.

For Macintosh:
1. For optimal display, we recommend that your monitor be set with 800 x 600 resolution.

2. Insert the CD-ROM into the computer's CD-ROM drive.

3. Double-click on the CD-ROM icon on the computer's desktop.

4. Double-click on the WorldView file within the CD-ROM window.

System Requirements

For Windows 98
- Intel Pentium processor – min 300 MHz
- 64 MB RAM minimum
- CD-ROM drive
- Monitor resolution of 800 x 600 or higher
- Sound card, speakers, and microphone

For Windows XP, 2000
- Intel Pentium processor – min 400 MHz
- 128 MB RAM minimum
- CD-ROM drive
- Monitor resolution of 800 x 600 or higher
- Sound card, speakers, and microphone

For Macintosh
- PowerPC processor – minimum 300 MHz
- MacOS OSX
- 64 MB free RAM minimum
- CD-ROM drive
- Monitor resolution of 800 x 600 or higher
- Sound card, speakers, and microphone

WorldView 2 Self-Study Audio CD

(This CD contains all the material for Student Books 2A and 2B.)

TRACK	STUDENT BOOK PAGE	WORKBOOK PAGE	ACTIVITY	
1			Audio Program Introduction	
2	3	14	Unit 1	Listening
3	3	14	Unit 1	Pronunciation
4	7	17	Unit 2	Listening
5	8	17	Unit 2	Pronunciation
6	10-11	20	Unit 3	Reading/Listening
7	13	20	Unit 3	Pronunciation
8	14	23	Unit 4	Pronunciation
9	15	23	Unit 4	Reading/Listening
10	23	28	Unit 5	Listening
11	25		Unit 5	Pronunciation
12	25	28	Unit 5	Pronunciation
13	27	31	Unit 6	Listening
14	29	31	Unit 6	Pronunciation
15	31	34	Unit 7	Listening
16	33		Unit 7	Pronunciation
17	35	37	Unit 8	Reading/Listening
18	37	37	Unit 8	Pronunciation
19	41	42	Unit 9	Listening
20	43	42	Unit 9	Pronunciation
21	44	45	Unit 10	Pronunciation
22	45	45	Unit 10	Reading/Listening
23	49	48	Unit 11	Reading/Listening
24	50		Unit 11	Pronunciation
25	53	51	Unit 12	Reading/Listening
26	55	51	Unit 12	Pronunciation
27	61	56	Unit 13	Listening
28	61	56	Unit 13	Pronunciation
29	65	59	Unit 14	Reading/Listening
30	67	59	Unit 14	Pronunciation
31	67		Unit 14	Pronunciation
32	69	62	Unit 15	Listening
33	71	62	Unit 15	Pronunciation
34	72		Unit 16	Pronunciation
35	72		Unit 16	Pronunciation
36	73	65	Unit 16	Listening
37	79	70	Unit 17	Listening
38	81	70	Unit 17	Pronunciation
39	83	73	Unit 18	Reading/Listening
40	85	73	Unit 18	Pronunciation
41	87	76	Unit 19	Pronunciation
42	87	76	Unit 19	Pronunciation
43	87	76	Unit 19	Listening
44	91	79	Unit 20	Reading/Listening
45	93	79	Unit 20	Pronunciation
46	98	84	Unit 21	Pronunciation
47	99	84	Unit 21	Reading/Listening
48	103	87	Unit 22	Listening
49	105	87	Unit 22	Pronunciation
50	107	90	Unit 23	Reading/Listening
51	109		Unit 23	Pronunciation
52	110	93	Unit 24	Pronunciation
53	111	93	Unit 24	Listening
54	117	98	Unit 25	Reading/Listening
55	118		Unit 25	Pronunciation
56	121	101	Unit 26	Listening
57	122		Unit 26	Pronunciation
58	124-125	104	Unit 27	Reading/Listening
59	125		Unit 27	Pronunciation
60	129		Unit 28	Pronunciation
61	129	107	Unit 28	Pronunciation
62	129	107	Unit 28	Reading/Listening
63		34	Unit 7	Extra Pronunciation Practice
64		48	Unit 11	Extra Pronunciation Practice
65		65	Unit 16	Extra Pronunciation Practice
66		90	Unit 23	Extra Pronunciation Practice
67		98	Unit 25	Extra Pronunciation Practice
68		101	Unit 26	Extra Pronunciation Practice
69		104	Unit 27	Extra Pronunciation Practice
70		107	Unit 28	Extra Pronunciation Practice